THE STERLING LEGEND

THE FACTS BEHIND THE LOST DUTCHMAN MINE

ESTEE CONATSER

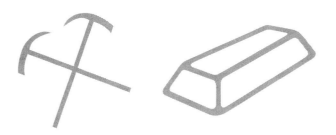

Gem Guides Book Co.
315 Cloverleaf Drive, Suite F
Baldwin Park, CA 91706

Copyright © 1972
Estee Conatser

Second Printing 1974
Third Printing 1979
Fourth Printing 1983
Fifth Printing 1987
Sixth Printing 1993
Seventh Revised Printing 2002

Published By: Gem Guides Book Co.
315 Cloverleaf Drive, Suite F
Baldwin Park, CA 91706

Cover Art: Scott Roberts

Library of Congress Control Number 2002104438
ISBN 1-889786-23-3

Dedicated

To

The Memory of Jacob Walzer

and

To

All Who Have Trod The Trails Of

Superstitions In Search of His

Fabulous Mine

CONTENTS

INTRODUCTION

This is the best book I have ever read relating to the Lost Dutchman Mine and I believe that nearly all Lost Dutchman Mine enthusiasts will agree with me. Conatser has used a cold-blooded approach to a remarkable assessment and analysis of this famous puzzle and has successfully attempted to clear the air of hundreds of confusing segments of the history.

Some of the legendary and mythical "facts", you will find, are conspicuous by their absence; and, yet, the author has, by innuendo and otherwise, given them their place in the history without mentioning them, directly.

I somehow feel that this book is a masterpiece because it can be read and studied by the fledging Lost Dutchman fan as well as by the fully-experienced and well-informed lost mine student and scholar.

Make no mistake about it, this will be a controversial book that will probably become the standard reference work. Nevertheless, the author has cleverly presented the pro and con of the Lost Dutchman in such a way that whatever the critics may say or think, this book cannot be used as a source of criticism. The author has simply, and merely, placed the known facts, the rumors, the innuendo, the legend, the myth, and the hearsay into an adventurous perspective. Actually, Conatser has done what hundreds of authors have attempted to do; give the questionable Lost Dutchman Mine legend a degree of proportion and a certain perspective.

To really appreciate this book to its fullest extent, you must place yourself in the author's shoes and try to determine how you would present the same facts, and still condense them into a book that would not be overloaded with boresome and extraneous matter. It is easy to imagine a book such as this, but the tedious task of sorting through hundreds of books, thousands of clippings, and thousands of reference cards and other products of research is something that the reader is rarely cognizant of and, usually, could care less. Having been in the author's files on several occasions and knowing that the author has dug deeply into the Exanimo library, I am sure that the author is one of the greatest living authorities on the Lost Dutchman legend. Barney Barnard lived in the shadows of the Superstitions for years, and he is gone. Barry Storm, in his time, devoted thousands of hours and several years of his life to the pursuit of the Lost Dutchman Mine, and he is gone. Bob Strait is gone, too, and he was, in his time, an intelligent and sensible searcher for the Walzer bonanza. Hardrock Hammond and I spent a fortune in time, effort, and expense in the pursuit of this riddle, and we both concluded that there never was a Lost Dutchman Mine — that the Dutchman's gold came from a cache of highgrade that he had secreted. Hammond is gone, too. So, the ranks of the old-timers who took a calculated fling at this legend are thinning out.

Then, there were dozens of other professional treasure hunters who shunned publicity and pursued their search with little regard for time or expense, and these are the ones we never read about, nor hear about. They went about their business in their own way, and capitulated with absolutely no fanfare. Most important of all, and Conatser has slyly mentioned it, they all failed.

But! many of those who failed in this pursuit were fortunate in finding something else. New interests, a new lease on life, greater intelligence, a fantastic recognition of nature, an incredible self-respect and self-reliance, and, among other things, an unusual new personal character. Then, there were, and are, those few that failure and disillusionment resulted in the instillment of pessimism and retaliatory objectives that, in essence, ruined their lives. Yes, the Lost Dutchman legend has disrupted many lives and altered or diversified nearly as many more. One thing is absolutely certain; had this book been in print 50 years ago, a great deal of the distress, confusion, disappointment, and failure could have been avoided. But, despite the definitive and objective purposes of this book, would it really have alleviated so much work and effort? Knowing the adventurous nature of both men and women as I do, I honestly doubt it. Much of the distress and disappointment would have been abated because the Lost Dutchman enthusiast would have been informed beforehand, if he would have read this book, of the odds and the stakes; and he would probably have plunged on ahead but on a different tack.

If you are a Lost Dutchman enthusiast or scholar, one reading of this book is not going to be enough. On second reading, I picked out ingeniously concealed figments of information that were authentic and, yet, unknown to me. This led me back to a third, and then a fourth, reading and on each trip I found that I had in my hands a refreshing riddle of reference material and data that made subsequent casual readings a wonderful literary experience.

The author, herself, is even more remarkable than this book. A treasure enthusiast of many years standing, an unusually adept researcher, a metal detector operator who is exceptionally skilled, and a far better-than-average author. She is a trusted friend and confident to many amateur and professional prospectors and treasure hunters, and one of the founders of the Prospectors Club of Southern California.

My first introduction came about too many years ago through a controversial exchange of correspondence with respect to the Lost Dutchman legend. By that time, I had exhausted my patience with this legend; while the author was yet probing and prying into the entire realm of Jacob Walzer. My pardner, Hardrock Hammond, succeeded in getting an appointment with her and reported that she was probably the best informed person available on the subject and suggested that we resume work on the Lost Dutchman. Since Hardrock and I still had some mining activities going and were completing some treasure projects, it was impossible to resume activity on the Lost Dutchman before his health broke and he passed on.

Later, among other things, our correspondence concentrated on metal detectors and I witnessed the author's progression from one brand and model through another until her critical and discerning nature caused her to settle on two models. You may have seen pictures of the author and her Master-Hunter in various newspapers and magazines. Both the author and her husband are successful coinshooters and their historical knowledge in treasure is above average.

As a researcher, she has few equals. She was one of the very first to understand and solve the LUE map and probably one of only two or three to interpret the IAYAYAM key. Her data files on the Southwest, Texas, Oklahoma, and Arkansas are probably among the most complete in the world. A hundred books could come from her files and 75% of the contents would be new material to the average reader or enthusiast.

Here you have a brief, superficial biography of the author and you have a sly, dependable, and thoughtful history of the Lost Dutchman legend. What you read, herein, is certain to be the basis for further books on the Lost Dutchman by future authors. No book, in my library, at least, has ever scrutinized a treasure story so objectively and it is certain that no treasure book has ever before taken such a definitive approach to the subject matter.

We need more books like this one, many more, and the publisher is to be commended for making this book available to the treasure hunting fraternity. Of course, many experienced prospectors will find this book a valuable reference work, too; and so will a lot of beginning prospectors.

One reading is not going to provide you with the entire message, so skim through this volume on the first reading — and then read and study on subsequent readings.

Karl von Mueller

Exanimo Hacienda
Segundo, Colorado
17 August 72

PREFACE

The Lost Dutchman Mine has been my own private madness for a number of years. In fact, over seven years have passed since I first entertained the thought of writing this book. But, like so many other things, it was always something I was going to do someday, and "someday" just never seemed to come. However, through circumstances and events every bit as incredible as the legend of the famed lost mine, the seeds of resolution and determination were firmly planted and this book was finally underway.

In my initial research years ago, I was appalled by the total disregard of some writers in keeping what few meager facts there were concerning the Lost Dutchman Mine separated from their own personal suppositions, assumptions, and, in some instances, down-right tall tales. In a treatise that is supposed to be dealing with truth or authentic legend, tall tales have no place. The suppositions and assumptions of others can be helpful when dealing with a subject of this nature, but ONLY when they are presented as such. Otherwise, they can be detrimental and cost the reader who pursues the subject many valuable research hours examining the 'facts' only to discover them to be someone's ideas or products of their imagination.

Despite some of the warped and fictitious material that had to be waded through, I finally managed to arrive at a conclusion that satisfies me. But the point is that had it not been for misleading information, that which took several years to accomplish could have easily been completed in one. Thus, the reason for this book; not to sell anyone on my own personal convictions, but rather to present a digest of the available information, discrediting that which cannot stand under close scrutiny and elevating the more worthwhile to its proper place. In other words, objectively separating the wheat from the straw.

For those seeking new clues or virgin information, they will find very little of either in this book. As previously stated, the primary purpose here is to study and review the existing information. Since a large portion of this is to be found in books that have been written over the past 30 years, for the most part, it is this material that will be presented and considered.

For you who are old hands in the pursuit of the Dutchman's gold, I hope that in this re-raking of old coals you will find at least one small spark that you missed or failed to consider before. And to the novice who is just beginning his quest, it is my sincere desire that this book will provide you with a good solid foundation for your research and that it will encourage you to think more for yourself, rely very little on the conclusions of others, and to accept nothing at face value.

There are several people who, in various ways, helped to make this book possible. First, I want to express my appreciation to my family for the patience and indulgence they extended to me while this book was being written. To Karl von Mueller, to whom I owe so much, goes my boundless gratitude. Without his guidance and council, this book would have never been written. Though he has now passed away, my sincere appreciation goes to Bill 'Hardrock' Hammond for his many words of encouragement and invaluable advice. I am also indebted to the late Bob Strait, whose life was ended all too soon. Too, I want to thank the staff at the U. S. Mint in Washington and the staff at the Bureau of Mines in Tucson for their cooperation.

As a last word, I want to quote a very good friend of mine who once told me: "The prerequisites for successful progress would seem to be, first of all, the facts — truth. And, secondly, the exercise of the most thorough reason. Enthusiasm and emotion should never be used as a basis for decisions. This does not mean that they have no place in the picture as they really do. They are a part of the facts which are to be considered when reasoning it out. In other words, the more a person teaches himself to reason and think, the more sound his convictions will be."

While this statement was made in reference to something else entirely, it is completely applicable and excellent advise to those who are seeking the truth of the Lost Dutchman Mine. I urge you to read it carefully and remember it well.

Estee Conatser

Los Angeles, Calif.
July 17, 1972

PROLOGUE

The myths and legends surrounding the legendary gold of Arizona's Superstition Mountains extend far back into the history of this savage but beautiful land.

Today, the mountains set in the midst of one of the most formidable deserts on the North American continent. But according to the pages of the past, there was a time when the area surrounding the mountains was rich and fertile, the home of an ancient civilization. It is from this all but forgotten time that the first tales of the fabulous riches of this mountainous mass of rock and twisted, tortuous canyons originate.

The Pima Indians have a legend that has been handed down from father to son for generations that tells of the mighty Montezuma, who reigned over the thousands of Indians that lived in the area. He had fabulously rich gold mines in these mountains that were worked using the slave labor of captives from enemy tribes. The legend discloses the many hardships endured by these slaves. They were never properly fed and each night were locked into cells in the compounds built near the various mines. As they died, they were merely replaced by others, and, in this fashion, so the story goes, Montezuma accumulated immense hoards of gold that he secreted in a cave that penetrated the bowels of the mountains. This continued for many years until one day Montezuma was overwhelmed with premonition of impending disaster. He herded the slaves and his people into the vast cave to await the predicted catastrophe. A terrible earthquake struck, ripping the land asunder. The entrance to the great cave was forever sealed. There, to this day, according to the legend, is Montezuma and his gold.

Myth? Of course! But what of the ancient ruins that were found in the late 1930's in the northern perimeter of the Superstition area by a group of men searching for the Lost Dutchman Mine? There was not much of a building remaining; in fact, just the stone foundation; in studying them, it was not difficult for the men to ascertain that the structure was large and had been divided by a long corridor, bordered on each side by tiny rooms, much like a present-day prison ward. I wonder if they ever heard the legend of Montezuma and his gold.

Spanish exploration of the Southwest began in 1536 when Cabeza de Vaca and his companion, a Moor named Estevanico, were found wandering in the desert by a small group of Spaniards. He told them of the fabulous riches of the Seven Cities of Cibola that lay far to the north. The famed Coronado expedition was formed to search for this fabled land. Months later, after discovering the Seven Cities of Gold to be nothing more than the mud pueblos of the Zuni Indians, Coronado was told of the colossal wealth waiting at Gran Quivira, an Indian pueblo far away. The disappointment over the discovery among the Zuni was replaced with anticipation, and with his eyes on the distant horizon Coronado began the journey. Again, instead of finding the gold he was seeking, he found another tribe of Indians living in mud huts and rooms carved into the side of cliffs.

The Spaniards were not easily discouraged, however, and many expeditions into the area north of New Spain followed Coronado's. Missions and pueblos were founded in remote areas and the infiltration of the Spaniards into the Southwest was underway.

From this era evolved hundreds of tales of riches buried throughout the Southwest, including the Superstition Mountains of Arizona. There are stories of the Spaniards using these mountains as a storehouse of treasure as far back as the 1600's. For one such story we revert again to the legends of the Indians, but this time the legend is of Apache origin.

According to the tale, many years ago a group of Spaniards coming down from the north ventured into the Apaches' sacred mountains (the Superstitions) in search of a suitable place to hide the many ox-carts of gold and silver bars they were transporting. They selected a cave near a prominent landmark, a tall sharp peak. Many trips were made in and out of the cave as they secreted their precious burden. Finally, all the treasure had been transferred from the carts into the cave and the entrance was then carefully sealed and camouflaged until nothing remained to indicate that a cave was there. The group then retreated from the mountains and were never seen again.

There is nothing to substantiate this legend; at least nothing verifiable. It is a fact that in the early years of the seventeenth century, the Spanish padres established missions in New Mexico and Arizona and attempted to Christianize the Indians. It is also a fact, though not often appearing in print, that along with their Holy duties, the Fathers carried on mining operations utilizing the labor of their Indian converts. According to some personal diaries kept during this period, just such mining activities took place near the pueblo of Santa Fe (the same Santa Fe that is now the capital of New Mexico). The Indians were ill-treated and suffered many abuses at the hands of their overseers. Finally, in 1680 there was a mass Indian uprising that caused the abandonment of many missions and pueblos, including Santa Fe, as the Spaniards, now hated, retreated south to Mexico.

There is an interesting story concerning the exodus from Santa Fe. It seems there was one group comprised of padres and soldiers who waited until the masses had vacated the village and then made a pilgrimage to the nearby secret vault where the gold that had been mined throughout the years lay hidden. They loaded the treasure into ox-carts and, making the desertion of Santa Fe complete, began their journey back to Mexico.

To avoid a possible encounter with Indians, they did not travel the usual route. Instead, they journeyed southwest into the desert wilderness seeking a suitable place much nearer Mexico to hide their fortune. Apparently they were successful because upon reaching Mexico the group from the Santa Fe pueblo had no ox-carts full of gold.

In a few short years, after several unsuccessful attempts, the Spaniards again had holdings, missions, and pueblos established in the Southwest. Their hold on this section of the country was fairly strong until the beginning of the nineteenth century when internal problems in Mexico began to take shape. In 1821, Mexico gained its independence from Spain. At the time, there were Mexicans who were successfully prospecting and mining in Arizona, among other places. The new-breed Americans had begun their explorations of the area. Sparks of struggle ignited into war between Mexico and the United States. The conflict, somewhat handily won by the Americans, secured Arizona and New Mexico as United States territory.

There are some accounts to the effect that when the United States gained possession of these border territories, many of the Mexicans furtively returned to the rich mines they had been working. They closed the mine openings so the Americanos would not find them, hoping that they or future generations of their families would someday be able to return. According to some, it was in this fashion that the mine known today as the Lost Dutchman came into being.

There are also tales which relate that during the mid-1800's the Apache, in his attempt to discourage the white man from over-running his homeland, covered up many rich outcroppings in and around the Superstition Mountains. And, later, stories to the effect that many of the fortunes in ore and bullion taken by the Apaches during raids and ambushes were hidden in various places throughout the mountains. There are those who maintain that it was from some of these caches that the famed Geronimo obtained the gold he used to buy guns and ammunition for warfare against the white man.

The influx of Americans into the territory began in earnest around 1850. Most of them were prospectors and miners, many of whom 'struck it rich'. As the word spread, more and more settlers came and towns such as Phoenix, Florence, and Tucson were founded. To protect the settlers from the marauding Apaches, the United States government established Fort McDowell, Camp Barrett, Camp Picket Post, Camp Pinal, and others. Very little time passed before stories began to trickle out telling of various individuals, soldiers, prospectors, and just plain cowpokes accidently discovering gold in the Superstitions. For one reason or another, however, none of them ever seemed to be able to return to the sites of their discoveries and work them.

It was in the early 1870's that the events began to unfold that gave birth to the legend of Jacob Walzer, the Dutchman, and his fabulous mine. Since that time a steady stream of prospectors and adventurers have poured into the area in search of this mine, each sure they could succeed where others had failed. The majority of them returned to civilization none the worse for wear. There were others, some say over 300, who met the grim reaper in bizarre fashions while searching for this elusive El Dorado.

So, the stories, tales, and legends persist and the searches continue. Like the Spaniards of long ago, the treasure hunter is an optimist and not easily discouraged — especially those obsessed with the legend of the Lost Dutchman Mine. Perhaps someday persistence will pay off for one of them. Just as there is no material proof that the Lost Dutchman Mine actually exists, neither is there any evidence to prove that it does not. Fact or fiction? Who can say with certainty?

"With reference to your letter of recent date, the Arizona Bureau of Mines has no factual information regarding the Lost Dutchman legendary mine. So far as we are aware, no commercial production of gold has come from within the main mass of the Superstition Mountains."

Associate Geologist
Arizona Bureau of Mines
January 14, 1965

"We know now that we stood before the greatest gold mine not only in Arizona, but probably in the United States. The whole region seems to be lined with gold-bearing ledges, some with bold outcroppings and others blind. Look out, however, for the Superstition gold mines, for they are going to astonish the world."

Excerpt from the Tempe,
Arizona News, 1893

Chapter One

The Alpha...

The beginning? It is difficult to determine exactly where to begin in trying to present the events, circumstances, occurrences that have transpired throughout the years to turn the relatively small mountainous mass known as the Superstition Mountains into one of the most intriguing, challenging, and deadly, yes deadly, regions of the American Southwest.

While it is difficult to ascertain where to start, the motive, or why, can be simply stated and summed up in one word – *Gold!* In addition to the discoveries of old ruins and diggings, there is ample amount of required history that enables one to state with certainty that white men were mining in the general vicinity, if not in the Superstition Mountains proper, well over a century ago. There is much evidence to back up the belief of many that these mining activities actually date back almost 200 years. Regardless of this evidence, it is interesting to note that during all this time, with the exception of the mines at Goldfield which lie in the desert at the western end of the mountains, there has been no known and recorded production of gold to come from the Superstitions or the immediate adjacent areas. The question is, why?

Are the mountains truly barren and void of gold as so many have maintained? And if so, what gave birth to the legends and stories of the fabulous fortunes of the Superstitions? Many legends were born long before Jacob Walzer left his native homeland on a ship bound for the harbor of New York. Could it actually be true? In spite of the thousands who have searched unsuccessfully, does a mine, or mines, containing riches that would stagger the imagination of man lie hidden somewhere in the remote vastness of the Superstitions? Could it be that it is not a mine, at all, but, instead, an enormous hoard of gold secreted in one of the mountains' many caves by the Spanairds or the fierce Apaches? Perhaps it is none of these, but merely a dream conjured by an imaginative mind or wishful thinking!

"In the beginning God created the Heavens and the earth" . . . . and so it was with the Superstitions. Geographically, the mountains are located in the Sonoran Desert of thee southwestern United States approximately 35 miles east of Phoenix, Arizona. They rise from an elevation of approximately 1,700 feet to the tallest peak, Weavers Needle; elevation 4,535 feet. While Weavers Needle is the highest peak in the main mass of the mountain, it is not the loftiest in the Superstition area. Tortilla Mountain, located a few miles northeast of the Needle, has this distinction.

There is very little about these mountains that is not controversial, including the boundaries. The names Superstition Mountain and Weavers Needle are practically synonymous, but, in reality, Weavers Needle is not actually a part of the main mountain, itself. Instead, it is situated 'behind' the mountain between Needle ånd East Boulder Canyons. When dealing with the Lost Dutchman Mine it is actually the Superstition area that is involved. For all practical purposes, this region is bordered on the north and west by the Apache Trail; on the east by Rogers and Reevis Canyons, and on the South by the mountain itself. There are some that will disagree with these boundaries but, nevertheless, for the most part it is this area that will be involved in this work.

The first question that usually comes to mind when one begins to think seriously of the Lost Dutchman Mine is whether or not it is geologically possible for a large gold deposit to be in the Superstitions. A quick trip through the more popular regions of the mountains will go a long way in convincing you that such is not possible. However, if you take a more leisurely journey and hike back into some of the more remote areas you may find indications that will make you stop and give it some serious consideration.

Then, in pursuit of the answer, if you were to gather together a dozen people, all proficient in mining and prospecting and well acquainted with the Superstitions, and ask them if gold deposits there are a geological possibility, chances are you would be able to sit back and listen to one of the great debates of all time. This is one of the major controversies concerning the Lost Dutchman Mine and one that has yet to be settled.

Is there Superstition Gold?

Gold is one of the most widely distributed of all the native elements and can be found in some degree in almost all common rocks. However, ore deposits containing enough gold to be profitably worked are rare.

Ore deposits were formed eons ago when masses of molten rock began to work their way up toward the surface of the earth. Some of these molten masses were thrust rapidly to the surface where they cooled quickly, not allowing the minerals and elements contained to separate. These rocks are called 'extrusive' and are uniform in appearance being comprised of grains so small that they are not distinguishable to the naked eye. These formations very rarely contain economically recoverable gold.

The 'intrusive' rocks are those which rose to the earth's surface more slowly and cooled within its mass. This slower cooling process allowed the minerals and elements therein to accumulate. It is from these formations and in zones of foiliated sediments that most of the workable gold deposits are found.

The richest gold deposits have been found in ore bodies that have received secondary enrichment. That is to say that after the primary

2

mass was cooled, liquids and gases found their way into the cracks and crevices and solidified, thereby forming veins. Some veins were also formed by cold water seeping into the rock from the surface, dissolving the mineral in one place and carrying it to and depositing it in another.

Due to the erosion of the earth's surface, many of the intrusive ore bodies are now exposed. From these outcroppings it is often possible to determine the type of minerals present in the lode lying beneath the surface. It is from these exposed ore bodies that most placer deposits are formed. Gold can never be broken down chemically, and it is the breakdown and disintegration of the surrounding rock, or matrix, that frees the gold which is then carried to stream beds and rivers where it concentrates with other heavy materials. This is a secondary deposit. Such "placer" gold is usually very fine.

Generally speaking, gold is most likely to occur in quantity in the intrusions of igneous rocks, and especially if the rock is relatively acid (light in weight and color). Some such rocks are rhyolite and andesite. Even though huge masses of intrusive rocks such as granite are usually barren of gold, valuable deposits have been found around the edges of such outcroppings. Huge formations of the basic igneous rocks, like basalt, rarely contain workable gold. The same is true for sedimentary formations. The metamorphic rocks, for all practical purposes, can be ignored by the prospector unless dikes or other indications of igneous intrusions are present.

A quick study of the geological maps of Pinal and Maricopa counties, in which the Superstition area lies, shows that while the region is igneous it leaves much to be desired insofar as favorable formations for gold are concerned. Almost the entire area is comprised of the extrusive rock, dacite.

There is a large section in and around Black Top Mountain that is completely basaltic, and while basalt can actually be either extrusive or intrusive, it is by no means favorable for gold. Just south and east of Weavers Needle is a formation of rhyolite which could possibly be gold-bearing. So could the small formation of andesite that occurs on the western and southern portions of the mountain, itself. The only dikes and plugs in the area are to be found at Weavers Needle and just east of the andesite occurrence on the southern side of the mountain. A fault, the only one in the area, bisects this formation and runs east and west along the southern flank of the mountain.

So, speaking from a geological point of view, there are very few areas that could possibly have ore bodies containing any appreciable amount of gold. And, the fact that these few possibilities have already been prospected unsuccessfully by hundreds of prospectors tend to discredit even these.

Further confirmation of this conclusion can be obtained by considering the geology of the Wickenburg (Arizona) region northwest of the Superstitions. Millions upon millions of dollars in gold has come from mines there and while many of the same type of formations occur, rhyolite, andesite, basalt, etc., there are other types of formations present that do not occur in the Superstitions and the total absence of dacite in the Wickenburg region is most obvious.

It is true that there are certain types of rock formations that favor gold deposits and others that do not, but in geology, as in everything else, there are exceptions to the rule. In South Africa there is a very unusual gold deposit which is found in layers of conglomerate that occurs in beds of sandstone. This unusual formation outcrops for over 30 miles — and, this 'exception to the rule' is the largest known gold deposit in the world.

The conglomerate consists of pebbles of white quartz and particles of gold in a matrix of quartz sand. Geologists believe that these are actually ancient placer deposits where the gold was deposited in layers, but the gold does not have the usual characteristics of placer gold and instead of the usual placer-type mining operations, it is mined using hard-rock methods. A good portion of the gold produced in the world today comes from this deposit and, according to reports, it will continue to produce for many years.

Ordinarily, the prospector can rely on the rules of geology, and must do so to be practical, but many a rich strike has been in freak deposits. For this reason the old proverb, *"Gold is where you find it,"* cannot be denied. The unanswered question remains: does such a freak deposit exist in the Superstition area? Someday, perhaps, someone will know the answer.

Chapter Two

Superstition History

How many people have died for gold?

The figure, one would guess after a second's thought, must be truly enormous. What is even more staggering, however, is the "lust-power" of that yellow element. It has literally turned men and women inside out, transformed them both mentally and physically. Gold has created wonders, and precipitated dismal depressions upon the human mind. Whether or not the search for gold is a virtue is not relevent to our case here. What is relevent, however, is that we, if not understand, at least recognize the overwhelming magnetism of gold. We shall view later how hard that magnet pulls.

The Lost Dutchman Mine has long been such a magnet, perhaps the largest of all for with it comes legend, and legends have tendencies to make men believe the unreal to be real; in a lighter, more humanistic vein, legends also exercise the span and scope of man's mind.

Jacob Walzer, the Dutchman, probably never realized what he started, or perhaps he did. For the Dutchman too gold's "lust-power" must have hit. Maybe he had dreams of even a larger mine, a sort of Dutchman's Lost Dutchman Mine. The basic fact remains: there is always another treasure for the treasure hunter ... no treasure, no matter how legendary nor profitable is *the* supreme discovery. Such be it with the mind.

But before we delve too deeply into the mentality of our subject matter and let ourselves also become engulfed with the power of gold, we must insert fact for fantasy.

In order to be able to properly evaluate the credibility of the many stories and legends pertaining to the Lost Dutchman mine, it is necessary to have a running acquaintance with the history of the portion of the Southwest that was involved. For this reason, the attempt will be made to condense hundreds of years of history in a few brief pages.

The first known civilized people to inhabit the portion of Arizona in question were the Hohokams, a tribe of ancient Indians whose culture and way of life was far advanced when compared to that of the more recent tribes. Chapter upon chapter could be written concerning these fascinating people, but that is not the purpose here. They will be dealt with briefly, however, because they are directly linked to the Superstitions and no history of the area, regardless of its brevity, would be complete without them.

As already mentioned, they were not savages. The Hohokams numbered in the thousands and, from evidence that has been found, the

5

center of their civilization was the Salt River Valley which is adjacent to the Superstition Mountains.

They were a very intelligent people. Where there was not sufficient water, they built an intricate system of canals which irrigated the arid land enabling them to grow life-sustaining crops. They had many villages throughout the valley. One, known today as 'Los Muertos' or City of the Dead, lies buried seven miles south of Tempe (Arizona) and has been of considerable interest to archaeologists.

The Hohokams lived in houses made of adobe mud, but in the Superstitions where rock was available their dwellings were constructed of stone and mud. The remains of these ancients' homes have been found throughout the Salt River Valley and in certain portions of the Superstitions.

As far as it is known, they had no written language. But many picture writings found on rocks and boulders in the region have been attributed to the Hohokam. They were very adept at using the materials supplied to them by nature and wove shoes, blankets, and other useful articles from yucca leaves, feathers, and fur. They made beautiful pottery and efficient tools.

While it may seem incredible, these people carried on mining operations. Some four miles south of Camp Verde there is a hill containing one of the essentials of life, salt. Recently, ancient tunnels have been found that follow the salt deposit through the hill. In these shafts, crude hammers and picks have been found dating back to the time of the Hohokam. Archaeologists, in their excavations in the Salt River Valley, have found little bells made of copper, indicating that they were also engaged, to some degree, in copper mining.

In the Garden Valley region of the Superstitions there are remains of some of the stone houses built by the Hohokam. Near the ruins there is an ancient Hohokam burial ground. Beautiful ornaments made of gold have reportedly been found in some of the graves. While being unable to authenticate these alleged finds, there is no reason to believe they are not true. If these ancient Indians had the ability and know-how to mine and utilize copper, it is likely that they could do the same with gold — if it was available.

An interesting story appeared in *The Phoenix Herald* in 1884. The story relates that two prospectors discovered a large hoard of ornately carved war clubs in a cave in the Superstitions. There were over 200 of these weapons which were very much like a policeman's night-stick, except much larger. They were carved from very hard wood and were found in a remarkable state of preservation. The article does not give the exact location of the cave nor does it tell what happened to the relics other than that the two men gave some of them to friends as souvenirs.

If this story is true, it would be interesting to know what happened to the bulk of these clubs since they would be quite valuable as relics on today's market. Actually, it would seen doubtful that the men would have removed them all from the cave simply because there were so many of them and, in those days, the significance of such finds was not fully appreciated.

In fact, from an archaeological viewpoint, the Superstitions are practically virgin. Almost everyone that has been interested in the area has been so busy looking for gold that they no doubt have overlooked many valuable relics and artifacts.

It is believed that the Hohokams made the Salt River Valley and surrounding area their home for over 2,000 years. Exactly when they disappeared from this region is not known. Their fate is unknown. Some say they were wiped out by disease, war, or some other disaster. Others tend to believe that they simply migrated to another area, possibly because of a continued drought. It is known, however, that when the Spaniards first came to the area in the mid-1500's their villages and houses were already in complete ruin.

Following the Hohokams to the area were the Pima and Maricopa Indians. Their origin has not been definitely established, but it is widely believed that they migrated from the north. There are some who maintain that the Pimas are direct descendents of the Hohokam, but, to date, this has not been definitely established.

Regardless of where they came from, they were a very primitive people whose culture could not compare with that of their predecessors. They exposed a live-and-let-live attitude, grew a few crops, dressed in loin cloths, and seemed to be perfectly content with their meager existence. When they came to the area is not known, but when the Apaches migrated there in the 1400's the Pimas and Maricopas were well established and already held the Superstition Mountains in awe and would not enter them.

The Apaches, according to their tradition which is to them what the Bible is to most of us, came to the area from Mexico. They had built up a fierce hatred for the Spanish conquerors since they had been forced from their native land, deep in Mexico, and for years had migrated further and further north in an attempt to escape the bonds of Spanish slavery.

The Apache was very different from his Pima and Maricopa neighbors, being nomadic and war-like. They would not stay in one place long enough to do any farming for themselves. What they wanted and needed in the way of crops, and almost everything else, they simply took by raiding and plundering the villages and dwellings of other tribes. Nor did they share the other Indians' fear of the Superstititons — not at first, anyway. They used the natural fortress as just that, a fortress. It was from these mountains that they would charge and attack the docile Pimas and Maricopas taking what they wanted, including squaws, and killing anyone who got in their way. Then as quickly as they had appeared, they would retreat back into the safety of the Superstitions where they knew the other Indians would not follow.

Shortly before the white man appeared on the scene, an event took place that caused the Apaches to change their entire attitude toward the mountains. There are contradictory versions as to the circumstances involved, but it seems that the Maricopas became thoroughly aggravated by the Apaches and their raids and decided to put an end to both. They set a trap, which, in the beginning, worked beautifully. After an initial battle, which sent the Apaches on the run, the Maricopas, their fear of the Superstitions replaced with determination to exterminate the band of Apaches, followed them into the mountains. However, the crafty Apache outwitted them and, once back into the mountains, ambushed the Maricopas.

There were many warriors of both tribes killed in the ensuing battle and even though the dead Maricopas outnumbered the dead Apaches, it was the greatest loss the Apaches had suffered in a very long time. Being superstitious, they held council and decided that the mountains were indeed inhabited by gods who had become angered because they had allowed the great battle to occur in their domain and, in revenge, had caused many Apache warriors to die.

In repentance, they decreed that the portion of the mountains where the battle occurred and the surrounding area was the home of their gods. It was a sacred area and was to be treated accordingly. From that day on, the region of the Superstitions from the western end, east to Weavers Needle and for some distance beyond was the land of the Apache Thunder God, and was taboo to any intruders.

As previously mentioned, the Spaniards first entered what is now Arizona in the mid-1500's. Soon after, they had established missions and pueblos as far north as Tucson. In the beginning they had no trouble bending the will of the friendly Pimas and Maricopas to suit their purposes and needs. After an initial friendly approach which allowed them to get fairly well established in the area, they began to force the Indians to do their bidding and work the deposits of gold and silver that had been discovered. If the Indian refused he was tortured or killed. Some of the Indians were taken prisoner and then transported to other areas or back to Mexico where they were sold as slaves.

It did not take much of this abusive treatment before the friendship originally extended to the Spaniards turned into hostility and revolt followed. Minor Indian uprisings occurred and the Spanish decided that if they were to get the most from the Indians they would have to approach the situation a little differently.

It was then, around 1580, that the Spaniards began in earnest to Christianize the 'savages'. They wisely relegated the labor to a basis the Indians felt was more voluntary. This system was called "reducing the Indian", and with the process the Indian was to undergo a ten year period of becoming 'civilized' during which time he would be converted to Christianity and taught the Spanish way of life. At the end of this decade, he would be declared a subject of the king of Spain; an inferior subject, no doubt, but a subject, nevertheless. In return for all these favors, the Indian would assist his benefactors in whatever work there was that needed to be done, including mining. It was in this manner that the mission system in this portion of the Southwest finally prospered.

Feeling their new northern boundaries secure, the conquerors, in their never-ending lust for land and gold, set their sights on the virgin land to the north. It was in the early 1600's that the pueblo of Santa Fe was founded and established as the capital of the new Spanish province called New Mexico. At the time, this included the area north of the Gila River in which the Superstition Mountains are located. During these early years of the Spanish era, the Church had much control over these new lands and the province of New Mexico was under the Franciscan regime while the land in lower Arizona, south of the Gila River, and other areas were under the rule of the Jesuits.

Except for the Apaches who, for the most part, were still an unconquered people and a constant problem, everything went fairly well for the Spanish settlers and missionaries. So well, in fact, that they began to slip back into their old ways of abusing their Indian converts. Ill winds began to blow. Finally, in 1680 the Indians' discontent erupted into a full-scale mass uprising. The end result was many dead Spaniards and hurriedly abandoned missions and pueblos as the rulers fled to the safety of Mexico.

It was in the late 1690's, after many abortive attempts, that they managed to regain their foothold in New Mexico and Arizona. However, the foothold was a shaky one and for the next few decades it was all they could do to hang on to their established holdings, so they made no attempt to expand into other areas. There is very little, outside of the mining operations conducted by the Spanish, that occurred during the following 70 years that is of particular importance here. It was in 1780 that the Jesuits were expelled, some historians say because they were hoarding the gold they were mining and not turning it over to the State as they were supposed to do. There is much evidence indicating that this is true. The Jesuits were replaced by the Franciscans, an action which caused a certain amount of internal unrest in the government. The turn of the 19th century found the Spaniards in a precarious position. Americans were beginning to make expeditions into the region, Mexico's internal problems were fast coming to a head, and the never-ending problems with the Indians continued, all making an already unstable situation worse.

Finally, in 1821 Mexico gained her independence from Spain. Arizona and New Mexico, naturally, became Mexican territory. This reign was short-lived, however, because early in 1846 the border disputes with the United States turned into a full-scale war. When it was over, the present international boundaries had been established. Arizona and New Mexico became possessions of the United States.

A couple of years later, gold was discovered in California – the stampede to the West was on. Apparently many prospectors were seeking gold as they traveled because many of them made rich strikes elsewhere and never reached the gold fields of California.

It was in 1863 that Heinrich Heintzel, an Austrian immigrant who had changed his name to Henry Wickenburg, accidently discovered one of the richest gold deposits in Arizona, dubbing it the Vulture Mine.

Other valuable deposits of gold, silver, and copper were discovered and by the time Jacob Walzer appeared on the scene, mining in Arizona was well underway.

But according to the fabulous legend, it is back in the early 1800's that the story of the Lost Dutchman Mine actually begins.

Chapter Three

Oro!

No treatise ever written on the Lost Dutchman Mine would be complete without the story of the original discovery of the mine. Since there is no recorded history, as such, regarding this, it is impossible to definitely establish how it all took place — if, indeed, it did. Of the many stories concerning this alleged discovery, the one presented here seems to be the most plausible when considering the history of the areas involved and the prevailing conditions of the times. This is not to say that this is the way it happened, but merely the way it could have happened.

Back in the early 1840's, there was a prominent Spanish family by the name of Peralta who lived in Sonora, Mexico. They were very well-to-do with most of their wealth being derived from a group of silver mines they owned and operated. The head of this household was Miguel Peralta. He had three sons: Pedro, Manual, and Ramon.

Miguel Peralta was getting old and with each passing day, he became more and more concerned over his family's future welfare. The mines that had produced so bountifully were almost worked out. He felt that before his death he must find a way to guarantee the family's future security. Mining was the only thing he knew and for him there was only one solution; new and profitable mineral deposits had to be located. After much serious thought and consideration, he decided the virgin land to the north was the most promising. Since his advanced years made it impossible for him to go, himself, he would send his three sons. So it was that the three brothers, accompanied by a small group of peons, began their journey. A journey that eventually led them to the Salt River in Arizona.

There, the sands of the river produced colors in their gold pans and, in the usual manner, they proceeded further and further upstream in search of the source. Eventually they arrived at a spot where there was a good concentration of gold (this place was later to become known as Mormon Flats). Here they set up a small placer mining operation and began recovery processes.

Once this was well underway, they turned their attention to prospecting for the deposit from which the gold was coming; the mother lode. After surveying the terrain, they determined that it was washing into the river from a nearby canyon that drained the rugged mountains to the immediate southeast. It was agreed that they must try to locate the deposit.

Pedro was in charge of the group that headed into the mountains, with Ramon and Manual remaining in camp to oversee the mining activities there. The group was gone several days and upon their return, reported success. They had located a deposit of gold so rich that it was almost unbelievable.

The three brothers immediately decided to return to Mexico and obtain the necessary equipment and supplies which would enable them to begin work on their newly-found bonanza. And they were very anxious to report the good news to their father.

Within a few months they had returned to Mormon Flats with the necessary men, equipment, and supplies. They reestablished the profitable placer operations under Ramon's command. Pedro led his other brother, Manual, and a group of workers to the fabulous deposit he had discovered on the previous trip and it was not long until mining there was in full swing and running smoothly.

Upon returning to the base camp at the river, Pedro rested for a few days and then, taking a small group of men with him, headed back into the mountains to investigate the possibilities of locating still more rich deposits. A few miles from camp, they encountered a canyon which drained into the creek they had been following. Here at the mouth of the canyon the waters flowed full and free over the small boulders. The area was unusually green and had a lush appearance; they gave the canyon a descriptive name – Fresco.

At this oasis-like spot they set up a secondary camp and began to explore the surrounding area. Again success was theirs; in Canyon Fresco they found another bonanza deposit. Within a few days they were busily involved mining the precious yellow metal. Most of the ore was so rich that it had to be worked by hand, and, in many instances, the gold could actually be cut out with a knife.

In close proximity another deposit was located, but this one was not as rich, making it necessary for them to build an arrasta to grind the ore. Even so, this deposit was by far richer than anything they had ever seen in Mexico.

In the meantime, back at the site of the first mine, they had discovered in the mountains, Manual had been doing some exploring and prospecting on his own and had succeeded in locating several more worthwhile deposits. Day by day, the amount of gold accumulated by the Peralta brothers grew at a fantastic rate.

The Apaches had been keeping a close eye on these white men and their activities. But since they seemed to be interested in nothing more than digging holes in the mountains and sands from the river bank, it was more a curious eye than a threatening one. There were comparatively few of them, the Indians reasoned, and there was no indication that they were an immediate threat to their domain. That, plus the fact that the Indians delighted in sneaking into the various camps at night and helping themselves to whatever happened to be available, made the intruders tolerable.

The Mexicans, on the other hand, were well aware of the Indians, but since they had been there for many weeks and outside of minor thefts the Apaches had made no hostile moves, the Peraltas decided they had nothing to fear. It was with a relaxed and happy frame of mind that they went about their work.

It was not long until they had amassed all the gold they felt they could possibly load onto the limited number of burros and mules they had with them. A meeting was called and the decision was made to return to Mexico with their precious burden and take a well-earned vacation before making another sojourn back to the seemingly inexhaustible mines which now, due to Manual's recent finds, numbered eight in all.

In preparation of their journey, with mixed emotions they discovered they had accumulated much more gold than they could possibly transport back to Mexico in a single trip. After giving the matter considerable thought, they selected what they believed to be a safe place and cached the surplus gold with intentions of retrieving it on their next trip. To make sure that in any eventuality the location of all the mines would be known to all three of them, Pedro drew three maps showing the location of each of the eight mines. Keeping one for himself, he gave the other two to Manual and Ramon.

The trip was an uneventful one and upon reaching their home, they found their father to be in very poor health and in a short time he died. The brothers then became involved in family affairs and settling their father's estate. The trip back to the mines was delayed longer than they had intended, but they were not too concerned. The fortune they had brought back with them was more than enough to keep the family in the style to which they were accustomed for several years and they hesitated to get back to the desert, the heat, and the work. Within a few months, Manual married his sweetheart and settled down to the business of establishing a family of his own. For the Peraltas, everything seemed to be well under control.

Not so for Mexico; the border disputes with the United States were beginning to take on serious undertones and it was not long before it was obvious to all that a war was inevitable. The Peraltas knew that if Mexico was defeated in this confrontation, the area where the mines were located would then belong to the United States thereby making it impossible for them to return and continue working the mines.

A family conference was hurriedly called to discuss the situation. It was decided they could not run the risk of waiting to see whether or not their country would be victorious; they would gather all possible men and supplies and return to the mines immediately to recover as much gold as possible before it was too late. Someone had to remain behind to look after family affairs and since Manual was the only one that was married, he elected to stay. In his place, a cousin named Gonzales would go.

Thus, a few weeks later the final expedition was underway. There were almost 100 men and twice that many pack animals. It was indeed a sight to behold and upon reaching the Superstition area, it was a sight that did not please the Apache. To them, such a large number of white men could only mean one thing – – – trouble! But in their usual manner, they bided their time and waited until everything was in their favor before making their move.

When they arrived at the site of their old placer operations, the expedition was split up into three divisions. One, under Ramon's command, remained at the river. A second, which was headed by Gonzales, was sent to work the mines in Canyon Fresco. The third group, Pedro's, went into the mountains and began work there. In their rush to recover as much gold as possible in the limited amount of time they had allowed themselves, all caution was tossed to the winds and they gave no thought to the Indians. This was a mistake that was to prove fatal.

A few short weeks later, Gonzales staggered out of the mountains and made his way to the camp at the river. He told of the horrible attack he and his group of workers has suffered at the hands of the Apaches in Canyon Fresco and how he, and he alone, had managed to escape.

Fearing a similar fate, Ramon sent a runner into the mountains to warn Pedro to gather his men and all the gold they had mined and return at once to the river. In the meantime, the Mexicans hurriedly packed the fruits of their placering operations onto burros, making ready for a hasty departure. Early the next morning, the two remaining groups were reunited. With all available pack animals heavily laden with gold, and giving no thought to the fortune they had stashed on their previous trip, they began their retreat. They were barely underway when the Apaches struck . . .

The battle raged for three days before the Indians finally managed to corner the expedition. And there, at the western end of the Superstitions, the Apache victory was complete.

A few days later many Indian squaws and boys were sent to conceal the Peralta mines to make sure they would never again lure the white man into their land. The process took only one month to complete, but when it was finished the job was a thorough one; not a single indication of the mines remained. That is, with one exception – a lone mine located high on the wall of a canyon and in such an out-of-the-way place that the Indians felt sure no one would ever find it. *This mine was left untouched.*

Unknown to the Apaches, there was one survivor of the massacre and, oddly enough, it was the cousin, Gonzales, who had managed to survive the initial attack in Canyon Fresco. After a tortuous journey, he arrived at the Peralta hacienda in Sonora, more dead than alive. He related the fate of the expedition, and swore he would never again go near the accursed mountains.

Shortly thereafter, the United States won its war with Mexico and took possession of the region that was to become known as Arizona. Manual, the only surviving brother, knew the mines of the Superstitions were lost to the Peraltas forever, and all but forgot the map he had put away so many months before – a map showing the location of eight fabulous gold mines.

And so goes the legend of the discovery of gold in the Superstition Mountains and of the men who paid the supreme price for the gold they wrested from the mountains. But, unfortunately, as far as it is known, legend is all that it is; there is not one shred of actual evidence to substantiate it. However, there are certain 'pointers' that are a matter of record, and, while there is nothing to directly connect them to this legend, the coincidences involved make them interesting to consider.

The name Peralta is a familiar one to any student of the Lost Dutchman Mine in that it appears in practically every story pertaining to the subject. It is also a name that occurrs repeatedly in the history of the Southwest and Mexico. First, there was Pedro de Peralta who served in Santa Fe, from 1610 until he was ousted in 1613, as governor of New Mexico . . . an area which, at the time, included the Superstition Mountains. There are a few hazy stories that have circulated for centuries regarding alleged treasures from the early Spanish pueblo of Santa Fe being hidden somewhere in the Superstitions. However, there is not enough available information available to even begin to try to ascertain whether or not there is any truth to these rumors. Nor is there anything in any of the stories connecting the one-time governor, Pedro Peralta, to the alleged treasures.

Then, according to some reports, the authenticity of which has been a matter of controversy for years, it was in 1748 that Ferdinand VI, King of Spain, in return for services rendered, granted 300 leagues of land in northern Mexico to one Don Miguel Peralta de Cordoba. Ten years later, this grant was extended further north to the Gila River and for some distance beyond. This, of course, was the famed and highly disputed Peralta Land Grant.

Upon Don Miguel's death in 1824, the land was bequeathed to his only son, Miguel Peralta II, who was born in 1781 in Cumpas, Sonora (Mexico). Apparently he had no sons, for upon his death the grant fell into the hands of an American cousin, George M. Willing, Jr.

It is unfortunate that the details surrounding the Peralta Land Grant have been so clouded and confused. In spite of court findings, it is all but impossible to get to the truth of the matter. Even so, there is nothing connecting the Peraltas, who discovered gold in the Superstitions, to the Peraltas involved in the disputed land grant. Of course, if one could be sure that the Peralta family who allegedly owned the famed land grant actually existed, it would prove that during the time in question there was a Miguel Peralta living in Mexico who was a wealthy land owner (Don Miguel Peralta's only son, Miguel II). However, whether they were for real or not, the Miguel Peralta of the Dutchman legend supposedly died in the late 1840's in Sonora, Mexico; Miguel Peralta II, heir to the land grant, died in 1868 in San Diego (California). One supposedly had three sons – the other had none! It should also be pointed out, however, that the name Peralta is a common one in Mexico but this in no way eliminates the possibility of the legend being true. It could have been an entirely different family of

Peraltas who discovered the gold in the Superstitions . . . and, the 'land grant' Peraltas could be entirely fictitious.

The name Peralta again appears in the history of this century. During the Mexican Revolution in the early 1900's, there was a General Peralta who served his government faithfully, and was executed by the rebellious forces.

While the story of Adolph Ruth will be dealt with in detail later, it is interesting at this point to note that it was from a Mexican general that Ruth's son, Erwin, obtained the map that later led his father on his ill-fated search for the Lost Dutchman Mine.

It should also be pointed out that there are some who firmly believe that instead of the Peraltas taking gold from the mountains, they carried an enormous hoard of the precious metal into the mountains. According to these reports, this took place around 1820 when Mexico was struggling to gain her independence from Spain and was executed by loyal Spaniards as a safeguard to make sure it did not fall into the hands of the revolutionaries. These sources further maintain that the Peraltas, who were in charge of the operation, made up the story of the mining expedition so they could get the gold out of Mexico without arousing suspicion. Instead of having their mules and burros loaded with mining equipment and supplies, they were actually loaded with the gold they were smuggling out of the country. Further, that once arriving in the vicinity of the Superstitions, they sent a large group into one region of the mountains to go through the motions of mining. In the meantime, Pedro and a select few found an appropriate site and secreted the gold. It was the group sent into the mountain on the fake mining operations that was massacred by the Apaches, while Pedro, his brothers, and the rest made it safely back to Mexico. In an attempt to substantiate this, they maintain that the death records of Manual, Pedro, and Ramon Peralta are on file in Sonora where they died and are buried, thereby disproving the story that Pedro and Ramon were killed in the massacre at the Superstitions.

Though it is difficult to determine the validity of this report, it is entirely possible that the alleged death records do exist. Just what they would prove is debatable unless there is some way to definitely establish that the Pedro and Ramon Peralta, to whom the death records apply, are the same brothers involved in the legend. At any rate, it is from this cache, they say, that Jacob Walzer obtained his gold.

In the midst of all the possibilities, probabilities, and legends, it is refreshing to be able to present a few actual facts of which there can be no doubt.

Exactly who, when, and the measure of their success is not known, but the fact remains that Mexicans did indeed engage in mining activities in the vicinity of the Superstition Mountains sometime before the United States took possession of the region. The proof of this comes not in the form of old records, but in the tangible form of the old mines themselves and other material evidence.

At Mormon Flats, which due to the construction of the Mormon Dam now lies beneath the waters of Canyon Lake, early pioneers found the remnants of early mining activities. At Government Well, a few miles northwest of Goldfield, there are ruins of stone buildings and an arrasta dump that date back to the Spanish-Mexican era. Two old stone corrals that have definitely been established as of Mexican origin have been found; one, near First Water Ranch just northeast of Goldfield, and the other located several miles further northeast near Mesquite Flats. Also located near Mesquite Flats are the ruins of an old arrasta and a stone house. These, too, are of Spanish origin. Definite indications of old Spanish encampments, including tell-tale Spanish drill bits, have been found on Tortilla Creek.

As far as the old mines themselves are concerned, there are several to be found in the region extending from Goldfield north to the Government Well area. The age of these mines has been established by Carbon-14 tests that have been run on the crumbling timbers that once supported the tunnels. They are of the Mexican era.

While being unable to verify it, one reliable source states that in the late 1930's a small group of men concentrating on the area east of Fish Creek, found an old tunnel about 8x8 feet in diameter that had been filled with river-run boulders that had to have been brought in from a considerable distance. They cleared the shaft down to approximately 15 feet where they encountered boulders so large that removing them would require blasting. Unfortunately, due to their financial condition, they were unable to buy the necessary powder. After unsuccessfully attempting to work around them, they gave up. According to this source, the shaft showed markings where green pitch from trees had been used to heat and split the rocks to extract the ore. This trick was often used by Mexican miners.

Extensive investigation by the group failed to establish what had been taken from the mine, but since the Mexicans were interested only in precious metals, the answer is obvious. Also, in the same area, they found an ancient trail, ore dumps, and stone ruins.

Establishing the fact that an area immediately adjacent to the Superstitions has produced a considerable amount of gold is easily accomplished by pointing out the discovery of gold at the western end of the mountains that led to the founding of the town of Goldfield. The deposit was discovered in 1890 by four Mormons who promptly sold the claim for a sizable amount of money. The deposit was successfully worked until it was pinched off by a fault. In attempting to relocate it by going deeper, flooding was encountered that no amount of pumping seemed to overcome. It has been reported that well over $1,000,000 in gold was taken from this mine. While this is not an extremely large production when compared to some mines, it nevertheless proves the existence of gold in the Superstition area, and but a mile or two from some of the old mines that were worked by the early Mexicans.

Back in the realm of possibilities and probabilities regarding other facets of the legend, it should be noted that during the time the first Peralta expedition was supposed to have taken place, the Indians were relatively quiet and peaceful, making it entirely possible that a small group of men could have carried on limited mining operations in the Superstition area without being molested by the Indians. It is also easy to understand why the Peraltas would have made one last big expedition to the mines because, in fact, the United States did gain possession of the territory involved with the signing of the Hidalgo Treaty in 1849. It would make good sense for Mexicans who had holdings in the area to make the most of them while they could.

In spite of the interesting points that, to a certain extent, parallel the legend, the fact remains that there is no actual proof substantiating the events as portrayed in the legend. And even though material evidence does exist proving that Mexicans were involved in extensive mining operations in the area immediately adjacent to the Superstitions, it is not known who they were or what the amount of their production was, and, in no way proves that their activities extended into the mountains themselves.

Nevertheless, it is a fascinating legend and threaded with enough historical coincidences and factual evidence to make it very easy for one who wants to believe, to do so. Who can say with certainty that, in essence, it is not actually an authentic account and due to the lack of records, the deaths of the principals involved, and the number of years that has passed, many of the pertinent facts have been lost ... somewhat like a jigsaw puzzle with missing pieces making the entire picture impossible to complete? This is something each and every student of the Lost Dutchman Mine must decide for himself.

Chapter Four

Apache Gold Hoard

It is well known that the Indians were most proficient in the art of concealing anything, mines and mineral deposits included; and they resorted to this time and again in many areas of the Southwest. Their object was simple: they knew the yellow metal attracted the white man, therefore, the more deposits they hid and mines they concealed the less there would be to lure the intruders into their homelands.

Once the Indians became fully aware of the value of gold and its importance to the white man, instead of discarding it when they found it among the loot they had plundered, they would take it and secret it someplace. This was not necessarily with the thought of using it themselves, but more over to keep it out of the hands of the Mexicans and Americans. No doubt there are hundreds of such caches hidden throughout the Southwest and, for the most part, if they are ever found, it will be by sheer accident.

This brings up another interesting facet to be considered when researching the Lost Dutchman Mine: did the Apaches know the location of gold in or near the Superstition Mountains? The answer is, yes, without a doubt!

Relative to this is the story of a Dr. Thorne who was probably the first American to set eyes on gold in the Superstition Mountains. Not only did he see it, but he came into possession of a very respectable amount of it and in a very unusual and almost unprecedented manner; he was led to it by the Apaches.

The versions of the circumstances involved leading to this rare event are as many and varied as those surrounding Jacob Walzer, but fortunately there is enough worthwhile evidence available to make certain the conclusion that the story is true. Time and space will not be taken here to relate the details of the many versions of the story, but it should be mentioned that they vary from one which has Thorne discovering a rich placer deposit while being held captive by the Apaches, to another stating that after curing a chief's wife he was led to a fabulous gold mine known as the *Pesh-La-Chi*.

Actually, it was in the early 1860's that Dr. Abraham Thorne, close friend and associate of the famed Kit Carson, served as army physician at Ft. McDowell, a military post located near the junction of the Verde and Salt Rivers in central Arizona. He was a well-known and respected man with both the troops and officers, as well as being very popular among the many Indians who often went to the fort seeking medical attention.

In 1865, Dr. Thorne's tour of duty was over and he began to make plans to return to his home in Lemitar, New Mexico. The news that the good doctor was about to leave the area drifted back to his Indian friends and they decided they would like to give him a token of appreciation for the excellent care he had given their people. So it was that they approached Thorne and told him they would like to give him a gift of gold but that he would have to go with them into the mountains to receive it. The Doctor was not quite sure what to think of the offer, but more to pacify them than for any other reason, he agreed to go.

A few days later, he met a group of Apaches at a predetermined spot near the fort and after submitting to a blindfold, Thorne was mounted on his horse, and with it being led by one of the Indians, the journey was underway. Within a short time, they crossed a river (which Thorne later said he believed to be the Salt) and continued on for a distance he judged to be approximately 20 miles. The party then halted, and after being helped from his horse, the blindfold was removed. Dr. Thorne saw a pile of gold lying at his feet.

He was told to fill his saddlebags and did so while furtively observing the area. Thorne later said that about the only things he could determine at that point was that they were standing in the bottom of a narrow canyon and that on a hillside he saw what appeared to be some sort of stone ruins.

After taking a portion of the gold, Dr. Thorne allowed the blindfold to be replaced and, in the same fashion as before, the return trip was underway. Before arriving at the point where the trip began, Thorne was able to ascertain that they were returning from the east and once, when his blindfold slipped, he was able to see the tip of a sharp peak to the south. After again crossing a river and reaching the vicinity of the fort, the blindfold was removed and after expressing his thanks, Thorne bid his friends farewell.

After this unexpected windfall, Dr. Thorne changed his plans and decided to go to San Francisco to sell his gold and visit close relatives there before returning to his home in New Mexico. It was a few years later that he returned to Arizona and began his now-famous search for the place where he received the unusual gift.

When all facts are considered, this is by far the most acceptable version of the story and the one that Thorne, himself, told a close friend. However, neither this nor any other version of the story can be definitely proven insofar as actual details are concerned. But, the fact remains that Dr. Thorne did sell an (undetermined) amount of gold in San Francisco for something over $5,000.00 during the time in question. And, it is a fact that a brilliant, well-educated, and respected man did spend a small fortune and many years in search of something in and around the Superstition Mountains and, according to Thorne, he was seeking the canyon where he received the gold from the Apaches.

In the final analysis of the Dr. Thorne episode there are a couple of points that should be brought out. First: Thorne, himself, was not positive that the Indians took him into the Superstition Mountains. While he believed this to be the case and spent most of his time searching in the Superstitions, it is entirely possible that the canyon he was seeking lies elsewhere. Second: it was not a deposit of gold-in-place that he was taken to, but a quantity of gold that had been brought to that spot and dumped on the canyon floor. The actual source of this gold is completely unknown. While it could have been taken from that very same canyon, it just as easily could have been brought in from several miles away. The one and only thing indicating that the source of the gold was nearby is the Indians' insistence on keeping Thorne blindfolded throughout both trips to and from the canyon. If the gold source was not nearby, it is difficult to understand why the Indians would have deemed this necessary. But this, of course, is mere supposition.

While there is only one point established by the Thorne story, it is an extremely important one. Whether it was an Spanish mine, a cache of their own or the Mexicans, or a virgin deposit, the Indians knew the location of the gold in the Superstition area and had access to it. There are several other stories from the same era indicating this, but since they do not provide any additional information that will be by-passed here.

Equally interesting are the stories concerning the Indians of today and their apparent knowledge of the location of gold in the Superstition area. Incredible as it may seem, there are a number of stories indicating this and while they cannot be authenticated, they are interesting to consider.

One such story tells of two Indian men who checked into a local motel at Apache Junction (Arizona) sometime in 1965. After spending a couple of days outfitting themselves, they made a trip into the Superstitions. Within a few days they returned, gathered their belongings, and after paying their motel bill, not in currency but in raw native gold, they promptly departed.

If this and other equally interesting stories can be relied on, it is evident that some of today's Indians are aware of and know where to find gold in the Superstitions – – – just as their forefathers did a century ago. In fact, there is very strong evidence supporting the belief of many that the Apaches are still, to this day, guarding the gold of the Superstitions. There are whispers of a mysterious band of Apaches known as the Black Legion who lives in the Iron Mountain region of the mountains and are there for the sole purpose of keeping anyone and everyone from finding a fortune in gold that is allegedly hidden near their sacred burial grounds. And while they are Indians, it is said that they are very modern and progressive. Instead of relying on the naked eye, they use powerful binoculars to keep a constant watch over the area where the gold is supposed to be hidden. And, in place of the old bow and arrow, they use rifles equipped with telescopic sights and in lieu of the crude knives once used, these Indians have 'graduated' to the machete and are most proficient in its use.

In past years, there have been more rumors regarding the existence of this clandestine group of Apaches, but, as the years go by, rumors are turning into a somewhat strong belief in some circles; namely, among those who have ventured into the Superstitions and encountered circumstances and conditions that lend credence to the stories of the Black Legion. It does, almost, seem impossible that they could live there in the mountains without anyone's knowledge, but, yet, anyone who has ever spent much time off the well-beaten paths of the region will know that it is not impossible . . . not in those mountains. Needless to say, the reports concerning the Black Legion should not necessarily be believed, but neither should anyone be foolish enough to disregard them completely.

But getting back to the days of old; it was a few short years after Dr. Thorne's experience that the stories of gold in the Superstitions were again flying fast and furious with the principal involved being none other than the Dutchman, himself!

Chapter Five

Enter the Dutchman...

Jacob Walzer has been called many things; highgrader, liar, drunkard, cheat, eccentric, and even murderer. On the other side of the coin, he has been described by some as honest, compassionate, kind man, and a victim of slander. His character seems to change as often as the details of the story of the Lost Dutchman Mine. This is mainly because many who have written about him tend to paint Walzer in whatever colors the author feels will be most compatible with his own version of the story.

Unless he was a veritable Jekyll and Hyde, he could not possibly have been everything he has been said to be. However, saint or sinner, he is responsible for one of the most fascinating and intriguing treasure stories ever to come from the American Southwest. For this contribution, he deserves a more prominent position in the annals of the great Southwest than the one he now holds.

Walzer is not responsible for the founding of a town, nor did he battle the Indians or outlaws, or accomplish any of the other deeds usually attributed to important or great men, but his achievement, in many ways, is nonetheless great. His contribution to posterity was very different; upon his death he left a legend. A legend that for almost a century has filled countless men and women with hope, plans, and dreams. Of course, the Dutchman's mine, if it is a reality, has eluded them all and they were unsuccessful in reaching their original goal. And, there are some who maintain that the only thing the search for this mine ever accomplished was to lead the searcher to bitter disappointment and, in some instances, death. However, you must remember that for every individual who has suffered because of the legend of the Dutchman's gold, a hundred have benefited from it. But instead of a fabulous gold mine, they found many of the intangible riches that no amount of money can buy.

The fortune for many lay in their discovery of the charm and magic of the desert; that incomparable hunk of Earth that gives so much to those who understand its beauty and tranquility. It was the challenge involved that led others to wealth in another form – – – the thirst for knowledge. In their pursuit, minds that were becoming siuggish and stagnating became active and alert. These individuals experienced many wonderful and worthwhile revelations that probably would have never been disclosed to them otherwise. Still others found the treasures that lie in dreams, hope, and optimism where they previously knew only drab reality and dejection.

The legend has indeed produced many incredible riches. And, it is this, the legend, that is the legacy of Jacob Walzer. A legacy that entitles him to a place of honor among the others that contributed much in making the early West into the fabulous era it was.

It is commonly accepted that it was around 1870 when the stories regarding Jacob Walzer and his mine first began to circulate in central Arizona. These stories are many and varied. In an attempt to seek out the truth, each one has been studied, pondered, and either discarded as sheer fabrication or set aside for further consideration. Needless to say, there were very few that were not eliminated. It is possible that some pertinent and worthwhile information was tossed aside in this process. If so, it is very unfortunate, but was unavoidable. What little information that was at one time available has been twisted, added to, subtracted from, and otherwise corrupted by various writers and individuals in their attempts to make all the ends meet, thereby enabling them to tie it all up in a neat little bundle (and this is something that cannot be done when dealing with the facts pertaining to the Lost Dutchman Mine), until very little remains for the serious researcher to work with. And, even these few remaining shreds leave much to be desired insofar as being information that can be relied upon completely and totally. At best, most of them are, merely strong possibilities, but they do warrant serious consideration by anyone seeking the truth.

However, there are a few facts pertaining to Jacob Walzer that are a matter of public record. These records state that it was in 1862 that a German immigrant named Jacob Walzer arrived in this country at the port of New York. According to reports that are commonly accepted as fact, he had been educated at Heidelberg University and, for 20 years prior to his arrival in the United States, had been working as a mining engineer in various countries.

Census records of 1864 indicate he was then living in Prescott, Territory of Arizona. Records said to exist in Washington, D.C. show that during the years from 1880 to 1889, Jacob Walzer shipped over $250,000.00 in gold to the U.S. Mint. Walzer died in October of 1891 following a lengthy illness and is buried in a cemetery in Phoenix.

These are precious few facts when considering that the man lived in central Arizona for over 25 years. Other than the stories pertaining to his mining activities, there are numerous other tales regarding his other activities, but like everything else concerning the man, these, too, have been clouded over and confused until it is all but impossible to know what is truth and what is not. A perfect example of this is the never-ending controversy over the Dutchman's character. Some maintain that he was a rip-snorting, hell-raising individual who committed murder to obtain possession of the mine and killed an undetermined number of people to keep it. Others say that he was a quiet, unassuming, and thoughtful man who, outside of a few close friends, kept pretty much to himself and came into possession of the mine in a completely legitimate manner. And, according to them, if he ever killed anyone it was most certainly in self-defense.

After having given this matter considerable thought, it is still difficult to understand why so much time and space has been devoted to this argument. Whether he was a bum or the very essence of goodness seems totally unimportant. The only thing that matters at this point is did he, or did he not, have a gold mine and, if not, where did he get his gold?

Since it is impossible to ascertain the truth surrounding Jacob Walzer and how he came into possession of the mine (if he did at all), the three most popular versions of the story will be presented. Even though one of the three seems more probable than the other two, one has no more authenticity than another, so you can choose whichever one suits your fancy with good chances that you will be as right in your conclusions as anyone else has been in theirs.

The first rendition states that in 1860, two prospectors, Ludi and Jacobs, were in a cantina in Mexico boozing it up when they met a man by the name of Manual Peralta. In the ensuing weeks, and over many shared bottles of tequila, the men became fast friends. One day, Manual brought the sad news that his father had died and that he must return to the family hacienda in Sonora to look after things. But before departing, he wanted to pass along some very important information that he had never told anyone before.

A couple of days later he took his two friends aside and told them how he and his two brothers, a decade or so ago, had discovered a group of gold mines in the territory of Arizona. He also told them how his brothers had been massacred by the Apaches, leaving him the only living soul who knew the location of the mines. He then presented them with a map and explained that it showed the location of eight very rich gold mines, and went into great detail giving them explicit instructions on how they could reach the mountains where the mines were located. He told them that he knew he would never be able to make use of the map or return to work the mines himself, and since he had no children to pass it on to, he wanted his good friends to have the information. He then said his good-byes and left town.

Apparently, Ludi and Jacobs did not have much faith in their friend or his information because it was not until 11 years later, in 1871, that they set out to try and find the mines. They followed the instructions Manual Peralta had given them which included mention of many landmarks such as La Sombrero Mountain, a black-topped mountain, specific canyons and tributary canyons, and they finally succeeded in locating one of the mines. It was as Manual had described; rich beyond imagination! They promptly began work.

In the meantime, another two prospectors, Jacob Walzer and Jacob Wisner, were prospecting near Florence (Arizona) when they decided to find out what the Superstition Mountains had to offer in the way of mineral deposits. They had spent a few days prospecting and exploring the area when late one afternoon they heard the familiar sound of a pick breaking rock. By following the sound up the canyon, they soon spotted two men working a mine high on the side of a hill. Without giving it a second thought, they raised their rifles, took careful aim, and fired, killing the two men.

The next morning they went to the mine and discovered its incredible richness. Walzer was overcome with greed and turning his gun on his pardner, he shot him dead. Then, he, and he alone, knew the location of the fabulous mine and there was no one to share it with.

According to the second version, which is short and sweet, Walzer was living in the vicinity of Phoenix with an Indian squaw who knew the location of a rich gold mine in the Superstition Mountains. However, for a long time, she refused to tell him its location. Finally, after much persuasion and assurance that he would protect her, she led him to the mine. Within a few days after their return to the Phoenix area, she was abducted by her fellow tribesmen who cut out her tongue for betraying a tribal law. But Walzer had what he wanted and leaving her to fend for herself, he went back into the mountains and began to work his newly-found bonanza.

The third story, while not being as exciting and full of violence, is the more acceptable of the three simply because the events as portrayed, to a certain extent, have actually occurred through the years to various prospectors. Though somewhat flimsy, there is some evidence backing up this version.

Around 1870, Jacob Walzer and Jacob Wisner were prospecting near Florence (Arizona) and ventured into the Superstition Mountains. They spent several days exploring the region with no luck whatsoever and were about ready to mark it up as a lost cause when they accidently stumbled across an old mine. Upon investigation they found it to be rich beyond anything either of them had ever imagined.

They wasted no time in beginning operations and before long it was necessary for them to return to Florence to buy more supplies. The gold they used to pay for their needed essentials caused whispers in the little town and before they left, half the population was aware of the two men and their gold.

It was a month or so before they again appeared in Florence. This time they had a quantity of gold they wanted to sell. After completing the transaction, they purchased more supplies and by the time they left town this time the word was out: the Dutchman and his pardner had a bonanza mine in the Superstitions.

A few months later, the Dutchman made a trip into Florence alone, leaving Wisner at the mine to continue the work. Upon his return, he found his pardner dead; the victim of a vicious Indian attack. Walzer, fearing to stay at the mine and work alone, buried Wisner and proceeded to camouflage the mine so no one else could find it. This completed, he retrieved a considerable amount of gold from where they kept it hidden and made a hasty retreat from the mountains.

From this point, most variations of the legend seem to coincide and, for all practical purposes, tell the same story. For the next decade or so, Walzer rarely went to the mine but each time he did, he would return with gold. It was these trips that fostered the portion of the legend that is so well-known today and tells of how the Dutchman, cleverly evading all who attempted to follow, would disappear into the mountains and reappear back in Phoenix a scant few days later with a burro laden with gold . . . ore so rich that it could be shipped directly to the mint without processing. And, though many tried, no one was ever successful in learning the secret of the Dutchman's mine.

The Superstition Mountains during a frequent afternoon thunderstorm.

WEAVERS NEEDLE. Many students of the Lost Dutchman Mine
believe this prominent peak to be "La Sombrero" in the many Spanish
treasure legends. There are other facts which support the opposite
conclusion. If this peak is the actual La Sombrero, many people believe
Walzer's mine should be located within a two-and-a-half mile radius of
its base.

Barry Storm, a giant in the treasure hunting fraternity, searched for the
Lost Dutchman Mine for several decades. Storm, who also wrote many
books on the mine, died in 1971. One of his books on the legend
became the basis for a motion picture.

The Massacre Grounds where the Peraltas allegedly met their fate at the hands of an Apache war party. This is also the area where Silverlock and Goldlock recovered more than $15,000 in gold.

Another view of the Massacre Grounds in conjunction with Superstition Mountain.

The author's "Mountain with the Mine," located on the east side of Tortilla Creek approximately one and a half miles south of the Old Tortilla Ranch. The upper arrow shows the Mine's location, the lower arrow and dot pinpoint the cave. Could this be the famous Lost Dutchman Mine? According to one Apache, the fabled mine is located in this area.

View from the "Mountain with the Mine." Dashed line indicates Old Spanish Trail, top arrow shows the location of a spring in the area, middle arrow locates the author's campsite and lower arrow points to Tortilla Creek. Many of the clues fit.

The author atop a boulder at Fremont Saddle pointing to East Boulder Canyon. In the background looms Weavers Needle and beyond it Needle Canyon where Adolph Ruth's skull was found in late 1931.

The entrance to Peralta Canyon. The trail twisting through this rugged canyon is believed by many to be the same one which the Peraltas traveled with the gold from their several mines. Near the mouth of the entrance is Don's Camp.

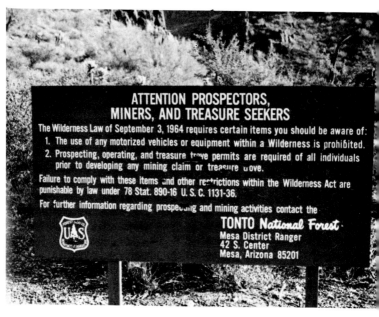

A warning to all would-be finders of the Lost Dutchman Mine. Notice the several bullet holes. Few people who enter the Superstitions go unarmed.

A peak along Peralta trail . . . with a little imagination it too looks like a sombrero!

A whittled saguaro cactus along Peralta Road. Some believe this cactus to be a marker pointing to treasure in the Superstitions.

A small hedgehog cactus, one of the many species of cacti which dot the Superstition wilderness.

Peralta Canyon. Note the sheer ruggedness of the terrain. It is little wonder why Walzer's mine has eluded its many seekers for nearly a century.

A very unusual rock formation on the east wall of Peralta Canyon. The arrow points to "Geronimo's cave." There are several informative books available on the geology of the Superstition area.

The Phoenix City Cemetery where Jacob Walzer's unmarked and uncared for grave is located, (reported to be lot 19, grave 4).

Chapter Six

Clues or Camouflage?

Probably the segments of the story of the Lost Dutchman Mine that have stirred the most interest are the legendary clues supposedly left by Walzer, himself. Many of these statements are, for all practical purposes, useless and will not be dealt with here. There are others that include mention of specific landmarks, descriptions, and other bits of information that would, on first impression, seem to be helpful to anyone seeking the mine. These will be delved into and after careful investigation and consideration an entirely different conclusion regarding the worth of these clues can be reached.

It is debatable whether or not Walzer actually made these statements, or whether they are merely tall tales dreamed up by someone long ago. Nevertheless, when dealing with this subject, no stone can be left unturned and each of these alleged clues must be analyzed to determine what, if anything, can be derived from them. For the sake of this study, they will be accepted as originating from the Dutchman, himself.

Assuming that Walzer made the statements, his motives for making them must be considered and kept in mind when analyzing them. This is necessary because many of his quoted remarks are confusing and contradictory, making them somewhat difficult to comprehend in some instances.

Ordinarily when someone divulges information regarding the location of something it is for the express purpose of informing the party involved of its whereabouts. There are reasons to believe that this was not Walzer's intentions and, if so, he failed miserably. If he were truly attempting to tell someone the location of the mine, it seems doubtful that he would have spoken in riddles which is the sum and substance of many of his clues. It is logical to assume that if he wanted to make the location of the mine known, he could have done so without difficulty. And, if he failed to accomplish this, it is most likely because he wanted to and had no intention of giving anyone enough information to enable them to find the mine.

It is possible that he could have been teasing his listeners by giving them part of the facts, but, perhaps, in a twisted or corrupt form. This, of course, would have been to pacify a somewhat warped sense of humor and for the satisfaction he might have derived in being able to sit back and watch them knowing they were all going in mental circles trying to figure out what he meant.

The third and most likely motive is that he partially or totally dreamed up the clues simply to quiet the inquisitive, or, perhaps, throw everyone even further off the right trail.

Regardless of his reasons, most authorities tend to believe that he actually made the statements and, while they are contradictory, difficult to understand, and, apparently, filled with hidden meanings, they still believe them to be legitimate hints to the location of the mine. Consequently, they must be presented and examined. The only logical way to go about this task is simply to take them literally. If there are codes or hidden meanings, they will be left for the cryptographer to decipher.

One of the most interesting statements attributed to Walzer is the one wherein he stated that no miner would ever find his mine. It can be assumed that he had a definite reason for using the word 'miner'. Otherwise, he would have used a word implying that his mine would never be found by anyone. With this in mind, he could have meant one of two things. First, that the mine was a freak deposit that no amount of ordinary prospecting methods would ever locate. And, secondly, he could have meant that it was not a mine at all. This, of course, would mean that instead of a mine, it was actually a cache from which he obtained his gold.

In further analysis of this statement and of possible help in ascertaining its meaning, the word 'mine' bears careful thought and consideration. The word has different meanings to different people. To some, a mine is one or a series of extensive man-made tunnels from which mineralized material has been taken. Others consider a mine to be any type of digging, from the shallowest prospect hole to an operation that extends for hundreds of feet. Webster, himself, has quite an assortment of definitions for the word. As well as the usual meaning, "a pit or excavation from which ores or precious stones have been taken," he also defines the word as "a subterranean passage" and "a rich store or source." It would be most interesting to know which was Walzer's definition.

In regard to the type of deposit, the Dutchman reportedly described it as being a chimney formation (deep and usually completely vertical) of rose quartz about 18 inches wide with the gold occurring therein. This conjures a mental picture of one of the most beautiful gold ores known. This ore, with the gold set in a matrix of rose quartz, is known as jewelry rock and is very much in demand by collectors today. While this type of deposit is more rare than some other gold deposits, they do occur and since there is no reason to believe otherwise, this description of the ore in the Dutchman's mine will be accepted.

Thus far, using the information contained in two of Walzer's quoted statements, it has been assumed that the Dutchman's mine was one of two things: a chimney deposit of gold-bearing rose quartz located in an area that would normally be void of gold with none of the usual indications present. Or, it was not a mine at all, but a hoard of gold that had been hidden at some time in the past by a party or parties unknown. While the latter, at this time, does seem to be a remote possibility, it, nevertheless, should be kept in mind.

True, this does not shed much light on the situation, but regardless of whether it was a mine or cache it appears obvious from these statements that anyone attempting to locate the mine by the usual prospecting methods is wasting their time and the only way they are ever likely to find it is by literally falling into it.

Regarding a cache, Walzer made another statement. He said that at the end of the day, he and his pardner would deposit the day's production in one of the three places where they kept their gold stored. He maintained that after the death of his pardner, he removed the two smaller caches but left the large one in place. As to the location of this site, he stated that you cannot find the mine without finding the cache and, by the same token, you cannot find the cache without discovering the mine.

This is a perfect example of one of his riddles and if anything is to be gained from it, it must be interpreted as is. In doing so, it has two possible meanings. One: they hid the fruits of their labor in or very near (within sight) of the mine and to find one is to find the other. The alternative is that once again Walzer was implying that the mine *was* a cache.

As to the location of the mine, there are several clues to be considered and examined. According to the Dutchman, the mine is located in an area of extremely rough terrain making it possible for one to be almost on top of it without seeing it. The mine, which Walzer described as being a cone-shaped pit, is supposedly situated in a ravine high on the side of a mountain with the mouth of the mine facing west. It is naturally hidden by the contours of the mountain making it impossible to see from below.

Directly across the ravine and facing the east is a rock formation shaped like a face that looks down on the mine. It is a short climb up to the top on the mountain from which the tip of a tall, sharp peak can be seen to the south. Also, across the ravine from the mine there is a cave. On the hillside below the mine, there is a horizontal shaft penetrating into the mountain. This uncompleted tunnel was supposedly started by the Mexicans when the pit above became too difficult to work. They attempted to tunnel into the deposit from the side in order to work the deposit more efficiently. Walzer said that he built a rock wall in the mouth of this tunnel to conceal it.

This seems to be a description of considerable detail regarding the mine and the immediate surrounding area. However, even if this is an accurate description, there is a good chance it is no longer applicable. In 1887, an earthquake of considerable magnitude ripped through the Superstitions and easily could have destroyed or altered all or part of these landmarks. In fact, in some places, tons of rock and earth gave way and were sent crashing down mountainsides making it entirely possible that Walzer's mine is now covered by half a hillside of dirt and boulders. However, on the other hand, it is equally possible that the earthquake left the mine unscathed and it is still just as the Dutchman left it so many years ago.

At this point, one naturally wonders about the date of Walzer's last visit to the mine. Was it before or after the earthquake? Unfortunately, this cannot be precisely determined. It is agreed, however, by most authorities that it was before the quake. So, there is no way of knowing if the mine was spared from the ravages of nature.

The clues Walzer left in the form of instructions on reaching the mine and some of the other pertinent information to be delved into is indeed a challenge. The challenge lies not in comprehending what he said, but in the attempt to ascertain if it is possible to apply his instructions to the topography of the Superstitions, and have them coincide with the landmarks he used as a guide. This is probably the most confusing and difficult portion of all the data that must be dealt with by students of the Lost Dutchman Mine.

According to the Dutchman, to find the mine you must go to the head of a deep, narrow, north-south trending canyon. The right canyon can be determined by the ruins of a stone house at its head. He further identifies it by stating that the old Military Trail runs along the bottom of the canyon and can be seen from the mine.

From this point, you proceed down canyon until you find a cave near the base of a high bluff. This cave faces north and at the entrance are the remains of a stone house, minus the roof, in which Walzer and his pardner lived while working the mine. With this cave located, you continue on down the canyon for a distance described as several miles, carefully observing the east side of the canyon. At an undetermined distance, you will see a rock formation in the shape of a face high on a ridge. This is the key. Directly across from this stone face is the entrance to the mine.

Now, before attempting to break down these instructions into segments for study, the remark he made in reference to the tall, sharp peak that could be seen to the south from the top of the mountain above the mine must be considered. As to the identity of this peak, there are three likely possibilities — Weavers Needle, Miners Needle, and Tortilla Mountain.

It is commonly believed that Weavers Needle is the peak referred to and this is extremely likely. It is situated almost in the center of the Superstition area and certainly fits the description.

Miners Needle is located approximately three miles southeast of Weavers Needle. While not being really comparable in height and prominence to Weavers Needle, it is a tall sharp peak and from certain portions of the Superstition area, it does serve as a very prominent landmark.

The final possibility is Tortilla Mountain. This is the highest mountain in the entire Superstition region and while it does not meet the description as well as the other two insofar as being a tall, sharp peak, when viewed from certain points it is equally conspicuous. It is located about 4½ miles northeast of Weavers Needle very near the northern boundary of the Superstition area. While both the Fish Creek and Tortilla Creek areas lie to the north of it, there are no real canyons,

31

as such, within the boundaries of the Superstition area north of Tortilla Mountain, so it can be eliminated.

In the end, we are left with Miners Needle and Weavers Needle as possibilities with no way of ascertaining, for sure, which of these is the tall, sharp peak that Walzer was referring to as being visible from the mountaintop above his mine.

From the Dutchman's instructions, the first prerequisite in finding the mine is locating the right canyon. The fact that it trends north and south is of very little help. There are at least nine canyons in the Superstition area that could be said to trend in a north-south direction. Fortunately, only three of these canyons have the distinction of having stone ruins at their heads (the key in identifying the right canyon). There are stone ruins at the junction of Fraser, Red Tank, and Randolph Canyons, but since they are so located, they have been eliminated; the description refers to stone ruins at the head of *a* canyon – not at the junction of three canyons. The three canyons that have stone ruins at their heads and trend in a north-south direction are La Barge, East Boulder, and Peters Canyon. If there are stone ruins at the head of any other north-south trending canyons, they are not known.

East Boulder can be logically eliminated because of its close proximity to Weavers Needle. From any point in East Boulder Canyon you are, for all practical purposes, almost on top of Weavers Needle and from a high vantage point could see a great deal more than its tip. Miners Needle, if it could be seen at all from East Boulder Canyon, would appear to the definite southeast.

La Barge and Peters Canyons are the two longest canyons in the Superstition area and both Miners and Weavers Needle would appear to the south from certain sections of both. In trying to determine which is the most likely, the terrain of each must be considered. Walzer described the canyon in which his mine was located as being narrow, deep, and extremely rough. This is where La Barge is eliminated. While it is a very deep canyon, it is not a narrow one! Quite to the contrary; for the most part, it is the most extensive canyon in the Superstition area.

Peters Canyon, the last possibility, does meet the specifications thus far. It trends in a north-south direction; it is deep, narrow, and very rugged. Both Weavers Needle and Miners Needle lie to the south of it and there are stone ruins at its head. Only one more requirement must be met; the old Military Trail must run along the floor of the canyon. It does not! The terrain along the bottom of Peters Canyon is so rough that it could not possibly support a trail and, in fact, it is almost impassable in places, even to foot traffic.

So, in attempting to follow Walzer's instructions to the letter, every canyon in the entire region has been eliminated. It must then be assumed that if Walzer was telling the truth, one of his specifications was in error. But which one?

Without being able to definitely identify the canyon in question, there is no practical way the remainder of his instructions can be followed. The cave in which he and Wisner lived would be the next major landmark to be considered, but without knowing which canyon it is located in there is no place to begin in ascertaining its location. Caves can be found throughout the Superstition area and the task of trying to find one particular cave without a single thing to go on is out of the question.

However, if newspaper accounts can be relied on, one man found it! An article (which will be presented in its entirety later) appeared in an 1895 edition of an Arizona newspaper stating that in 1894 a man named Bickell "stumbled upon the ruins of a stone house in the mouth of a large cave." The article does not give the location of the cave other than that it was in the Superstition Mountains. The article went on to state that the man was never able to go back to the cave because he could not find anyone willing to grubstake him for the necessary supplies needed to make the return trip.

Actually, there seems to be some disagreement regarding the distance from this cave to the mine. According to Walzer's statement, the mine was located a few miles down canyon from the cave in which they lived. But he also mentions a second cave which was located directly across the ravine from the mine. But there are some who believe that there was only one cave involved, and that it was the one located directly across from the mine. They maintain that it was in this cave that the Dutchman and his pardner lived. This idea was probably fostered by information that came from other stories, but, when dealing exclusively with information that was supposed to have come from Walzer, himself, it can only be concluded that there were two separate caves. Regardless of whether there was one or two caves, when and if the cave containing the stone ruins is located, careful exploration of the canyon involved coupled with thorough and systematic searching with modern electronic equipment should produce the mine − if, in fact, there is a mine.

In summarizing Jacob Walzer's clues to the location of his mine, every one of the conditions he described is present in the Superstition area, but not *as* he described them. Interpreting these clues as they have been reported leads one exactly nowhere. It is at this point that Walzer's motive for passing out these clues is all important.

If he was honestly attempting to tell the location of the mine, he undoubtedly made at least one mistake in his instructions. Or, the reports regarding these statements are in error. Nevertheless, with proper exploration which would probably take years, there is a slim chance that one of the key landmarks might be found thereby putting you on the right trail. However, if he lied about the clues for whatever reason, no amount of searching for key landmarks is going to pay off.

Since there is no way of knowing for a fact if he was misquoted or mistaken about one or two details or if he was lying about the entire matter, in preference to spending month upon month looking for

33

landmarks that may not exist where they are supposed to, it is by far wiser to simply disregard them completely and seek other sources of information pertaining to the location of gold in the Superstitions with the hope that as research continues, perhaps some of the other information will coincide and tie in with the Dutchman's clues making it possible to partially utilize it then. If not, it is best forgotten.

Before departing from Jacob Walzer and his 'contributions' to those who seek his mine, however, there are a couple of things that should be pointed out. First is the all important fact that only a few days would pass from the time he would leave Phoenix until he would return with the gold. The distance to and from the mountains is approximately 70 miles. How far he had to travel into and out of the mountains is not known. He was an old man who made these journeys alone and had no help in recovering the gold. Considering these facts, it is obvious that about all Walzer had time to do was go to the site and just literally pick up the gold, perhaps camp over night, and return to Phoenix. In fact, he reportedly made statements to this effect many times. He simply was never gone long enough to do enough mining to produce the quantity of gold he returned with.

Since as far back as 1916 there have been persistent rumors to the effect that Walzer highgraded his gold while working at the Vulture Mine near Wickenburg (Arizona). In fact, there was a man known as the Dutchman who did, for a while, work at the Vulture Mine. But, it is very doubtful that this man was Jacob Walzer. The Vulture employee lived in Wickenburg and as far as anyone knows, Walzer never lived there. But the one thing that really blows a hole in this theory is the fact that the richest ore ever produced at the Vulture ran $100,000 to the ton. For Walzer to have highgraded the $250,000 worth of gold that he shipped to the mint, he would have had to steal 2½ tons of the richest ore the Vulture ever produced. Need more be said?

That he had a source of gold in or near the Superstitions there can be very little doubt. Just what this source was and where it was are puzzles. It could be precisely as the legend states: an extremely rich deposit located in an area where gold ordinarily would not occur. It is equally possible that it was not a mine at all, but a cache of gold hidden years before by either the Indians or the Mexicans. As to the location, there is nothing but the never-ending question mark.

Regardless of the clues that do not fit, the hundreds or thousands of unsuccessful attempts that have been made to find it, cache or mine, somewhere in those mountains or the immediate surrounding area is the source from which the Dutchman obtained his gold.

Chapter Seven

The Two Soldiers

Though Jacob Walzer is the most famous, there are others who have allegedly found gold in the Superstitions. But, unlike the Dutchman, most of them were never able to recover any of it. The stories regarding these discoveries range from those without any evidence whatsoever to back them up, to others that have a great deal of authenticity.

In addition to a couple of the more worthwhile accounts that will be presented here, some of the other stories, though lacking evidence to substantiate them, will be dealt with briefly because they tie in and are in accord with the more substantial reports.

One of the most intriguing of all took place in 1880 and involves two soldiers from Ft. McDowell. After being discharged, they traveled from the fort to the town of Pinal where they intended to look for work. After making inquiries in town, they went out to the Silver King Mine to talk to the manager, Arron Mason, to see if he had anything to offer.

Even though the two boys had no mining experience, Mason seemed to be more than anxious to help them and their interview developed into a somewhat lengthy conversation. One of the soldiers mentioned to Mason that in order to economize they had not taken the stage to Pinal but had hiked the entire distance. And, in an attempt to shorten the trip, they had not taken the usual route via Apache Trail but had taken what they thought would be a more direct route — across the mountains. Both soldiers agreed that this had been a mistake for in doing so they had encountered extremely rough terrain, making the trip a very difficult one.

It was then that the boys remembered the peculiar ore they had picked up on the way at an old mine dump they happened to pass. They showed a piece of the ore to Mason hoping he could tell them what it was. He could and did: *gold!*

Very surprised at this information, they gave the bag containing the rest of the ore to Mason. Upon examination of the ore, Mason estimated that they had approximately $600.00 worth of gold. He then went on to explain to them that it was very rich ore and asked them if they thought they could find the dump again. They replied that it was a cinch because a short distance from the old mine dump they had encountered an old trail that led them south, past the tall, sharp peak that they had noticed while at the dump gathering the ore. From there, the trail led them down into an east-west valley, across a few canyons, past a ranch, and, finally, to the main trail leading to Pinal. On the advice of Mason, they decided to return and stake a claim.

The following day they were paid over $700.00 for the ore and after purchasing adequate supplies and turning over some $300.00 to Mason for safe-keeping, the soldiers left town to return to the old mine dump. They were never seen alive again. A few days later, the nude body of one of the soldiers was found in a shallow grave near the trail leading up toward Miners Needle. He had been shot in the chest.

Even though the body of the other solider was never found, it was concluded that both had been shot and killed by someone who, no doubt, was following them. Apparently the boys discovered that they were being followed, recognized the party and, therefore, had to be killed. The crime was never solved.

By using a topographic map and the description of the soldiers' route out of the mountains, it is possible to backtrack a portion of it. And, since the character and reputation of Mason and his superintendent, Robert Bowden, who was on the scene and backed up Mason's story, was excellent, it is worthwhile to do so.

Beginning at Pinal, the main trail runs west along the south side of Queen Creek to Whitlows Ranch. Here it crosses the creek and intersects with the stage road from the Silver Queen mine. A few miles past the ranch, an old trail veers off to the north with the stage road continuing on to the northwest. The trail continues north for several miles and then enters a small east-west valley in which it crosses three small canyons before beginning its ascent that leads up past Miners Needle. It is here at Miners Needle that their route is lost.

Just past this peak, the trail forks. The left fork leads to the northwest past Bluff Springs and into La Barge Canyon. The right fork takes off in an eastern direction for about one mile and then makes an abrupt turn to the north, past Whiskey Springs and Picacho Butte where it, too, runs into La Barge Canyon. There are so many trails running into and out of La Barge, and in all directions, that it is impossible to figure out which one the two soldiers were on. Actually, there is room for doubt that it was any of these trails that the soldiers followed.

The La Barge Canyon region is, and always has been, one of the most well-known regions in the Superstitions. This causes a certain amount of doubt as to how the soldiers could have been in this area without knowing their whereabouts. When relating their experiences to Mason they implied that, for all practical purposes, they were lost until they encountered the main trail leading to Pinal. There is one other trail that they could have used and while it does not pass directly by Miners Needle, it does pass within close proximity.

In the little valley where the trail previously outlined turns to the north, there is another trail that continues on to the east to Randolph Canyon. Here, it turns in a northern direction up Red Tank Canyon. Near the head of Red Tank it veers off to the northwest, crosses La Barge Canyon, and continues north past the head of Peters Canyon, on beyond the base of Tortilla Mountain and finally runs into the Apache Trail near the summit of Fish Creek Hill.

The portion of this trail, north from La Barge Canyon to Apache Trail, is one of the oldest trails in the entire Superstition area and is known as the Old Spanish Trail. Without a doubt, this trail leads to and through some of the most rugged terrain to be found in the area. This could have very easily been the trail the soldiers found after leaving the old mine dump where they found the rich ore.

Trying to approach the problem from another angle, or the place where the two soldiers entered the mountains after leaving the fort, is equally baffling. It is not known precisely where they left Apache Trail and took off on their short-cut across the mountains, but there are only three ways that offer fairly easy access into the Superstition area from the Apache Trail. One is Willow Springs. It leads over into West Boulder Canyon and on over into East Boulder Canyon where there are trails leading in all four directions of the compass. The second is La Barge Creek which, naturally, leads into La Barge Canyon and to many other trails, including the ones that lead to Miners Needle. The one other place where they could have easily entered the mountains is at Tortilla Creek where it crosses the Apache Trail. Here, they could have followed the creek to its junction with Peters Canyon and, from there, either proceeded on up the creek to its head, or they could have taken the more direct route up the canyon to its head. Either way, they would have encountered very rough terrain and would have run into the Old Spanish Trail that leads south and, finally, into the small valley south of Miners Needle. It is anyone's guess as to which, if any, of these routes they used.

The only thing definite that can be derived from this episode involving the two soldiers is that they entered the Superstitions from an unknown point on Apache Trail, found gold ore, and emerged from the mountains at Miners Needle. The most important facet is that the boys allegedly found the ore on an old mine dump, thereby adding substance to the possibility of the existence of an actual gold mine in the Superstition Mountains. While no material evidence remains to prove the validity of this report, there is very little room for reasonable doubt that it is true. Too many reputable people saw the ore and talked to the principals involved, and no one had anything to gain by lying.

In conjunction with the saga of the soldiers and their discovery is the story of Joe Dearing, who allegedly found this same mine dump. While there is nothing to give it a truly authentic flavor since the story comes from Dearing and there is nothing or no one that can verify it, it is nonetheless interesting.

In 1881, Joe Dearing appeared in Pinal seeking a temporary job while waiting for the arrival of his pardner. After this, Dearing had plans . . .

There were no openings at the Silver King Mine and while waiting for one, he went to work in a local saloon for a man named Brown. Soon employee and employer became good friends and, soon after, Dearing confided in Brown and told him of his plans and why he was so anxious for his pardner to arrive – – – he had found the mine dump and the mine where the two soldiers, the year before, had found the rich gold ore. Once his pardner arrived, they were going to begin to work it.

Naturally, Dearing would not reveal the location, but he did tell Brown that the mine was a pit-type digging that narrowed with depth and was now partly filled with rubble. He went on to explain that penetrating the hillside below the mine, there was a tunnel with a walled-up entrance. (If this sounds familiar, you are right. It coincides exactly with a portion of Walzer's description of his mine. It bears pointing out that Dearing related this description to Brown in 1881 — ten years before Walzer's death and almost that many years before the reported clues left by Walzer were public knowledge.)

The only information Dearing would give Brown regarding the location of the mine was that it was in an area of extremely rough terrain. When asked how he managed to find it, Dearing said that after hearing the story of the two soldiers he figured there should be a trail leading to the mine and that he simply followed the directions given by the soldiers.

Shortly after this conversation, Dearing went to work at the Silver King Mine. After making friends with his foreman, John Chewning, he told him virtually the same story he had told Brown. But, he produced a piece of ore he had taken from the dump for Chewning and added one additional bit of information. He said he had found the mine and dump by following an old trail and remarked that before reaching the mine, the trail became somewhat tricky making it necessary to go through a *hole*. Exactly what he meant by this no one seemed to know.

Unfortunately, Joe Dearing did not live long enough to make his anxiously awaited trip back to the mine. He was killed in a cave-in at the Silver King a week or so after his conversation with Chewning. If Dearing did find the mine as he said, he took the secret of its location with him to the grave.

Among many others, John Chewning made numerous attempts to locate the mine, but was never successful. It is, of course, possible that Dearing was lying to both Brown and Chewning and could have obtained the piece of ore he showed Chewning from any one of several sources. But if so, when considering the time element involved, it is remarkable, to say the least, that his description of the mine coincides exactly with Jacob Walzer's.

Another story that coincides, somewhat, with that of the two soldiers was reportedly related by an aging Mexican woman named Maria Robles. According to this report, she stated that when she was a very young girl she went with her sweetheart, Juan Gonzales, from Sonora to a very rich gold mine in the Superstition Mountains. She further stated that they went, at a time when the Peraltas were not working the mine, for the purpose of highgrading gold.

To reach the mine, she said that they followed an inclining trail past a tall peak, and, from the top, the trail went down over a slope and on to the mine. According to Maria, the gold occurred in grain-size particles and was taken from a deep, vertical, cone-shaped digging.

This story lacks authenticity of any kind and has been presented here only because the descriptions given coincide so closely with others that are from more reliable sources.

Maria's sweetheart was named Juan Gonzales; the name Gonzales appears in another interesting story which is supposed to have taken place in 1874. This Gonzales went by the name of Ramon Peralta Gonzales and, according to the story, he came to Maricopa (Arizona) from Mexico and was seeking someone to grubstake him. For some reason, he decided to approach the local telegrapher.

Gonzales told his prospective pardner that he had a map that was given to him by his father, Manual Peralta, shortly before his recent death. He went on to explain that his father had told him that many years before, he and his brothers had taken "mucho oro" from Canyon Fresco which was located in the mountains south of Four Peaks – the mountains that included La Sombrero. Gonzales told the telegrapher that the map showed the location of Canyon Fresco and the mine.

After much haggling, the telegrapher was allowed to see the map briefly and ascertained that the canyon in question drained from the mountains, northwest into the river. An undetermined distance from the river, the canyon forked to the east and to the south. At this fork, on the map, there were markings indicating that the mine was near.

Gonzales finally was successful in getting his grubstake and after buying supplies, so the story goes, he proceeded up the south bank of the Salt River seeking the remains of two arrastas his father said could be found near Canyon Fresco. But he never got that far; along the route, he stumbled upon the site of the massacre where he found several decaying bags filled with gold. Not being of a greedy nature, he was well satisfied with his find and abandoned his search for his father's mine.

This story, for whatever it is worth, gives the first indication as to the location of the famed Canyon Fresco. When relying on the telegrapher's description of the map, Canyon Fresco could be none other than Tortilla Creek.

It is the only remarkable tributary that runs into the river from the Superstition Mountains and forks in the prescribed manner. The first fork on Tortilla Creek occurs at the point where La Barge Creek drains into it. This is near Mormon Flats, and while it is well-known that the Mexicans did carry on placer operations here, there has never been any reference made relating to a mine being in this immediate vicinity.

Further up Tortilla Creek, a second fork occurs at its junction with Peters Canyon. Here, the creek continues on to the east, forming the left fork, with the right fork being formed by Peters Canyon which, at that point, leads to the south, matching the fork on the map exactly.

There are many people who believe that La Barge Canyon is Canyon Fresco, but, evidently, there are a few things they have failed to consider in reaching this conclusion. No doubt the fact that the Mexicans maintained a camp and mining operations at Mormon Flats influenced their thinking to a certain extent; what they failed to consider is that La Barge Creek is actually a tributary of Tortilla Creek, and while La Barge Creek does form what could be considered a south fork at its junction with Tortilla Creek, it was placering operations that were carried on in this area, not hardrock mining. There is also the obvious fact that La Barge Creek (or Canyon) does not drain directly into the Salt River. Canyon Fresco, according to Gonzales' map, does.

There is also the fact that there has been considerable evidence found at Mesquite Flats indicating that hardrock mining was carried on in this vicinity. There are the remains of an old stone house, a corral, and the ruins of a tell-tale Mexican arrasta, all within a scant mile or so from the junction of Peters Canyon and Tortilla Creek. Also to be considered is the name the Mexicans gave the canyon. The word 'fresco' implies abundant water, cool shade, etc. This description comes much closer to describing conditions on Tortilla Creek at and near the junction with Peters Canyon than those on La Barge where it runs into Tortilla Creek. At this point, the previously mentioned remains of the old Mexican encampments and old Spanish drill-bits that have been found near Tortilla Creek in the Tortilla Flats area, almost a stone's throw from the mouth of Peters Canyon, should be remembered.

All things combined, it is reasonable to conclude that Tortilla Creek is Canyon Fresco and that the fork shown on the Gonzales map could very likely be the fork formed by the junction of Tortilla Creek and Peters Canyon. Nevertheless, it is possible that the junction of La Barge Creek and Tortilla Creek form the fork shown on the map. Possible, but not probable. It should be remembered, however, that the entire story of Ramon Peralta Gonzales and his map is questionable and should be considered as such. It should also be remembered that it could be true; there is nothing to prove that it is not.

There is another story involving a map, and, while the circumstances involved are contradictory to the accepted version, it does come from a reliable source and could be true. For this tale, we must go back to the time when Walzer and his pardner, Jacob Wisner, were still working the mine.

According to most sources and the accepted version, Walzer's pardner, Wisner, was killed by a group of Indians at the mine while Walzer was in town buying supplies. Walzer found his body upon his return to the mine and buried it nearby. There is another version that tells a little different story: Instead of actually being killed by the Indians, Wisner was fatally wounded but managed to crawl a considerable distance in search of help. According to this rendition, the Pima Indians found him and took him to Dr. John Walker, a well-known and highly respected man.

After treating his wounds, the doctor gave Wisner a sedative and hoped for the best. The next morning it was obvious that Wisner was not going to live, but he was conscious and able to talk. He reportedly explained to Walker that he had been attacked by Indians at his mine in the mountains and went on to say that since he had no living relatives, he wanted the doctor to have his map showing the location of the mine. He then produced a rawhide map and soon after giving it to the doctor, he died.

Shortly after, Dr. Walker married an Indian girl whose people led him to a rich silver deposit that later became known as the Vekol Mine and made the doctor a multi-millionaire. The old map Wisner had given him was all but forgotten, but the doctor did show it to one man, Tom Weedin, a newspaper editor, who was allowed to copy it.

According to Weedin, the map showed the Superstition Mountains with a canyon draining northwest into the Salt River. The map also indicated that in this canyon, there was a small tributary canyon running into it from the east side (could this be what Walzer described as a ravine?). The gold mine was marked as being near this small tributary.

There are at least a dozen similar stories, but none of them offer much in the way of additional information and since they are one-of-a-kind without coinciding with any other story, they will not be presented. The stories that have been dealt with are interesting and, in most instances, bear enough authenticity to warrant serious consideration. But when using the word 'prove' in the truest sense, they do not prove anything. If you choose to believe that all the men who related these stories and presented them as true from personal knowledge (Mason, Brown, Chewning, Walker, Weedin, and the others) were lying, then they, most assuredly, are worthless. It is, however, most difficult to believe that all of these men (who, for the most part, were very prominent individuals) were liars. Some perhaps, but not all. Nevertheless, the decision to believe or not to believe them is yours.

Chapter Eight

Key Landmarks

Landmarks have been used forever in guiding people to almost any and everything, including gold. In researching the enigma of the Lost Dutchman Mine, mention of the same landmarks is encountered repeatedly in the material. In an attempt to establish if anything worthwhile could be derived from the comments pertaining to the prominent features of the region, they were compiled and tabulated. This crude tabulation produced nothing astounding in the way of results, but it was interesting and shed a certain amount of light on the situation in general. Time and space does not allow for a complete dissertation regarding this tabulation, but the highpoints will be discussed.

The one landmark that seems to stand out from all the others and is mentioned in almost all the stories concerning gold mines in the Superstitions is a tall, sharp peak. And, invariably, this peak is always located some distance south of the mine, or where the gold was found. It has been commonly accepted, by most people, that this peak is Weavers Needle. It is, for a fact, one of the most prominent landmarks in the Superstition area and certainly is a tall, sharp peak. But, according to the various stories, none of the principals involved in the stories ever mentioned the peak by name. This opens the door to the possibility that it might not be Weavers Needle, after all.

According to available information, Weavers Needle was named after the French trapper and explorer, Pauline Weaver. He first ventured into what is now Arizona in 1832 and, 30 years later, was a member of the party involved in the discovery of the rich La Paz Placers near the Colorado River. He was also instrumental in locating several other rich gold deposits in Arizona. He died in 1866 while serving as a scout at Camp Verde.

It is not known, for sure, when Weavers Needle was given its name, but a topographic map dated 1900 identifies Weavers Needle as such. Chances are that the name had been used for decades before this and probably even before Weaver's death.

As mentioned in an earlier chapter, Miners Needle or Tortilla Mountain could have been the peak referred to in many of the tales. Miners Needle, when compared to Weavers Needle, is certainly not as prominent, but one must consider that when compared to the terrain of the surrounding area, it does, indeed, stand out as a tall, sharp peak. And, while Tortilla Mountain could not honestly be described as a tall, sharp peak, it is the highest mountain in the Superstition area and is topped by a rugged, rocky peak. From certain areas, it is as conspicuous as Weavers Needle.

All in all, from most reports, the only important thing regarding this peak is that the mine is located somewhere to the north of it. Regardless of which of the three peaks they were referring to in the stories, it makes very little difference because "somewhere to the north of it" is of very little help in locating the mine.

Before leaving the subject of mountains and their relationship to the gold of the Superstitions, it should be mentioned that in many stories pertaining to the original discoveries of gold in the Superstitions, a mountain called La Sombrero marks the vicinity of the gold deposits. Many maintain that this, too, is Weavers Needle, but this is doubtful.

The name itself, La Sombrero, implies that the mountain was hat-, or sombrero-shaped and Weavers Needle simply does not fit this description when being truly objective. There are two mountains in this section of Arizona that do bear this name: one is in the Galuiro Mountains of Pinal County and the other is located near Cherry Creek in Gila County. The Mexican's La Sombrero could be either of these two or a mountain that is presently nameless, or known today by another name. Incidentally, Tortilla Mountain could be said to have a sombrero-like shape.

Trails also play an important part in the legends and stories concerning the Lost Dutchman Mine. In fact, according to some reports, there is a trail that leads directly to the mine. However, if there ever was such a trail it has, no doubt, been obliterated by now.

The Superstition area is literally full of trails that twist, turn, and lead in all directions. There are three, however, that could be considered more prominent than the rest and are probably the first main trails to ever penetrate the area. One is the old Military Trail that was used by the soldiers as a route from Ft. McDowell on the Verde River to Camp Pinal, near the head of Queen Creek. The second is a trail which leads from the mouth of La Barge Canyon through the mountains and emerges at Miners Needle. Third, there is the Old Spanish Trail which is most likely the oldest of all. As previously stated, it extends from La Barge Canyon, north to a point on the Apache Trail near Fish Creek Hill; a distance of approximately ten miles. This trail is easily traced and visible today. Of course, there is the Apache Trail, but it skirts the mountains and does not penetrate them.

No, there is no shortage of trails in the Superstition area and this, in itself, is the problem when trying to use the information involving trails as an aid in locating the mine. There are just too many to even begin to ascertain which ones are pertinent and relative to the legends and stories. It is possible to make some educated guesses, but that's about all.

The canyon in which the mine is allegedly located would be one of the most helpful landmarks of all, if there was a way to know for sure which canyon it is. This matter of the canyon has already been dealt with in considerable detail in an earlier chapter, and, in review, it is only necessary to mention that it is supposed to trend in a north-south direction, extends for several miles, and has the ruins of a stone house at its head. When considering this information exclusively, there are two likely possibilities: La Barge and Peters Canyons. This is not to say that others do not deserve consideration.

Of the most important landmark of all, the mine itself, if it does exist, there is this much known: it is located in a ravine high on the side of a canyon wall, or mountain. It is a funnel-shaped pit located in an area of extremely rough terrain and can be reached from a long, north-south trending canyon. It is very likely hidden, either naturally, by man, or both.

So, in the final analysis, all the landmarks combined and the information derived from all the stories does not pin-point a specific region where the mine should be found. In almost every instance, there are at least two possibilities for each landmark and no way to definitely eliminate either. In other words, they lead to nothing more than a blind alley.

Chapter Nine

Across from a Cave...

As you may have noticed, caves were not included in the group of landmarks just reviewed. This is because they warrant special attention since the only established worthwhile discoveries that have been made in the Superstitions have been made in caves.

The stories regarding caves in the Superstitions would almost provide enough material for a book. First, of course, there is the cave in which Jacob Walzer and his pardner lived and the cave that was directly across from the mine. These have already been discussed and will not be dealt with again. Instead, new and more intriguing food for thought will be introduced.

The saga of Geronimo and his battle against the white man is well-known and a matter of history. However, there is one facet of the Geronimo story that is not so well-known. This concerns an immense amount of gold that Geronimo allegedly had hidden and used to buy guns and ammunition. There are some reports that place this cache as being located in various places, all the way from New Mexico to the Sierra Madre Mountains of Mexico. And, yes, some say it was in the Superstition Mountains.

According to one story, after Geronimo had been captured and was being held prisoner in the stockade at Ft. Sill, Oklahoma, he attempted to bribe a guard into releasing him by offering to tell him the location of a vast quantity of gold. In order to whet his appetite, Geronimo supposedly told the guard that the gold was buried in a cave in the Superstition Mountains of Arizona. The key to the location of this cave, Geronimo allegedly said, was a rock formation in the shape of an Indian's head. The cave was located directly under the 'nose' of this stone Indian. The guard was not stirred by the information (due to Geronimo's trait as a well known liar) and when this became obvious, Geronimo would say no more.

Though this story has been reported as fact by some writers, there is no evidence to back it up, and it must be treated accordingly. Nevertheless, it is a story that this writer is very fond of, in that it supplied me with a couple of very exciting hours.

On one trip into the Superstitions to check out a theory, quite by accident a rock formation as described by Geronimo was found. This formation, which rose to a height of approximately 100 feet, was situated in the middle of a canyon with nothing else around it and was shaped perfectly into the profile of an Indian's head, similar to the one on the old buffalo nickels. After a short but rough climb, a shallow cave directly under the 'nose' of our stone Indian was, indeed, found.

Needless to say, at this point the tension was mounting. Unfortunately, extensive investigation and careful checking with metal detectors failed to produce even the smallest particle of gold. If this was the place where the great Geronimo had secreted his gold, it has, as stated in Stevenson's *Treasure Island,* "been lifted." For anyone who might be interested, this rock formation, which, incidentally, faces the east, is located in Peters Canyon about one mile up the canyon from its junction with Tortilla Creek. There are numerous other caves to be found in this canyon.

It is unfortunate that time and space does not allow for the presentation of all the interesting and entertaining reports involving caves in the Superstitions, but they are simply too numerous. For various reasons, four of these stories have been selected to present here for your consideration. Three appeared as articles in Arizona newspapers; these will be presented in their entirety.

The first comes from a 1916 edition of the *Phoenix Gazette* and while it is little more than entertaining, it is that!

"During the fall of 1913 Jose Perez, a Mexican, although born and raised in Phoenix, was on a prospecting trip in the Superstition Range. One day while riding down the bottom of a rocky bottomed rugged canyon, whose sheer walls towered far above him, he noticed a slight indentation in the rocky sides about 200 feet up from the bottom, which appeared like an entrance to a small cavern. Curiosity overcoming him, Perez investigated and struggling to the spot, discovered a small dark opening about 2 feet in diameter which seemed to lead directly into the mountain. He wriggled into this opening for a distance of about 20 feet when the cavern suddenly opened into an immense chamber. From this chamber a large passage in which a man could walk upright led into the heart of the mountain. By the aid of a number of matches which he fortunately carried, Perez was enabled to follow it back for a considerable distance, passing through several chambers like the first one. In one of these chambers reposing on a flat rock the Mexican found several nuggets of high-grade gold placed in the form of a dagger or stiletto. Above this on the rocky wall of the cavern were some rudely drawn cabalistic signs.

"The now thoroughly excited Mexican hurried from the place and mounting his horse rode over the hills to Miami, where he told his tale to a mining engineer, Roy Thomas, in whom he had the most implicit faith. He declared that he believed the 'Lost Dutchman', about which he had heard many tales, had been discovered.

"Gathering together the necessary equipment for exploration, Perez and Thomas, accompanied by a newsman, returned to the scene of the discovery, where a thorough investigation was made. The cavern led back into the mountain for about 200 yards but no visible indication of mineralization was evident, although some signs of previous occupancy was present. The mouth of the cavern was so small and situated at such an angle that only by the greatest accident could it be discovered from the bottom of the canyon. Thomas and the writer

returned to Miami while the disappointed Perez wended his lonesome way.

"A couple of years later Perez was in Phoenix a greatly excited and much scared Mexican. Lured by the call of gold and unable to forget the previous experience he had returned to the cavern and there, to his amazement, on the same flat-topped rock in the cavern chamber reposed some nuggets of gold in the shape of a dagger and above it rudely drawn into the rocky walls the sinister sign, 'Keep Away. Death'. Below was the rude drawing of a dagger. The Mexican, thoroughly frightened, immediately left the cavern and hurried to Phoenix and then, to cap the climax, last night as he was walking down the street, a form suddenly emerged from the darkness, thrust a paper into his hand and then as suddenly disappeared. When the frightened man reached the light and opened the missive it contained a crude drawing of a knife with the following words: 'Stay away from the Superstitions'.

"Whether all this is merely a gigantic hoax on the part of a practical joker or whether, indeed, through the mysterious veil of the past, there looms up the magic and sinister ghost of the 'Lost Dutchman' is a matter of further discovery. At any rate, Perez will in the future stay away from the Superstition Range and its mysterious warnings."

Needless to say, this is quite a tale. Perez probably did locate a cavern, but once inside its deep, dark recesses he allowed his imagination to get the best of him. As far as the mysterious encounter on the street is concerned, this was probably someone's idea of a joke.

According to the article, the symbol Perez repeatedly encountered was the drawing of a dagger. Extensive research has produced only one other source of information where such a symbol is encountered. In the 1950's, some ancient stone tablets were found near the Superstitions. Photographs of these tablets show that on one of them, among many other signs and symbols, there is carved an intricate drawing of a dagger. It is possible, but very doubtful, that there is a connection between the two; primarily because Perez's reported experiences are somewhat difficult to believe.

The second article is from a Globe (Arizona) newspaper, *The Miami Silver Belt,* and appeared in the October 16, 1913 edition. Strangely enough, it connects a cave with a deposit of rich gold ore. While such articles cannot be depended upon completely, there is much food for thought in this one, and especially when keeping in mind some of the stories that have been dealt with in previous chapters.

"H. A. Sidow returned to Globe after the exploration of the entrance to the cave described by Pete Moranga, the French-Mexican prospector, during his recent visit to Globe. It was the descriptions and samples of gold running from $5,000.00 to $50,000.00 per ton which caused so much excitement among the members of the Mexican colony and started the stories to the effect that the Lost Dutchman Mine has been found.

"Sidow says that while he is not willing to go on record to a statement that Moranga is on the track of the Lost Dutchman, he is willing to say that Moranga has discovered a good size cave in a remarkable formation, the mineral found somewhat resembling bismuth. This mineral is not ordinary bismuth, but even if it was bismuth, this in itself would not discourage old-time prospectors since gold is often found in conjunction with bismuth.

"Sidow says that Moranga is not willing that he should make public the location of the cave since he is anxious to make further locations in that immediate locality without taking the general public into his immediate confidence. But he is willing to talk about the general features of the cave itself and the chances for the finding of the gold.

"I have often noticed the spot where Moranga showed me the entrance to the cave,' said Sidow. 'As I have been prospecting for gold in the mountains and as I have been looking for the Lost Dutchman, I have passed the place many times; but I never thought about it as the entrance to a cave'.

"Moranga claims that it was at the entrance to this cave that he several weeks previous had found pieces of the black rock supposed to be bismuth. Moranga picked up the four extremely rich specimens of gold. The entrance of the cave is located about 25 feet above the level of a creek bed and it might easily be by-passed by any person not thinking of the existence of a cave in that immediate vicinity.

"I did not start out with Moranga on this trip. But I did meet him as he was returning from a prospecting tour. He willingly offered to show me the cave, provided I would not tell anyone where he picked up the gold samples. He was very frank about the matter and said he was not satisfied in his own mind that the gold had come from that immediate district. But he wanted more time to explore the country and he ask me to promise not to reveal the location of the cave.

"The time that Moranga discovered the cave and the gold, he went into the mine only a few feet. The entrance to the mine is so small that a fat man could not crawl through it. I started to go in head first, but after I had crawled a few feet I did not like the looks of the thing and not knowing where I might land I crawled out again. Then Moranga started in feet first and I crawled in after him, also feet first. After we had gone in about 25 feet the entrance commenced to widen to a diameter of 100 feet, I should say. Then again it would narrow.

"It was not the abandoned workings of a mine I am satisfied, but rather the entrance to a cave. I examined it as carefully as I could to determine whether or not we had stumbled into an old mine. At times the floor was so uneven that we had the greatest difficulty getting over some of the obstructions. Then at times the cave would run in a zig-zag sort of fashion.

"The walls were of limestone and we picked up some specimens of what resembles bismuth in some respects. There was a great deal of guano on the floor. Towards the last of our explorations the ground commenced to get wet and for this reason I am satisfied that there is *lots of water there. We did not go as far as we might have gone for the reason that we were not equipped for exploring a cave and either one of us might have taken a sheer drop of hundreds of feet downward without warning. I should not have objected to going further into the cave if we had been equipped with ropes. But without ropes it appeared to be taking too great a risk. However, we did get 3 or 4 hundred feet into the cave without reaching any end to the opening in the ground. The air was fairly good and from that it might be argued that there was another entrance somewhere besides the one we found.*

"I have turned over the piece of black rock or bismuth which I found over to an assayer and I expect to have a report on it soon. I do not believe that the black rock will show any traces of gold. But I do believe that Moranga found that black rock and the specimens of gold at the entrance to the cave just as he said he did. One man's guess as to where the gold came from is just as good as another man's. It would be interesting to follow the cave to the end for it must cover a good lot of country and might strike into a different formation. It is possible that Moranga stumbled on one way that the Lost Dutchman or some other dutchman came out with his ores. Again we might have run up against a solid stone wall a dozen feet from where we stopped. Moranga can throw no light on that situation for I went in with him farther than he had ever been alone."

In this article it is interesting to note that Sidow, who apparently was an experienced prospector and knew from his own examination that the tunnel was a natural cave, referred to it in one instance as a mine. This is a perfect example of a person using one word when he actually means another. It does indicate that at least one miner used both terms, 'mine' and 'cave', in reference to the same opening in the earth. No doubt that it is this type of loose wording that has contributed much to the confusion surrounding the Lost Dutchman Mine.

At first glance, the following article appears to be nothing more than an often-told tale that has been re-hashed and perhaps elaborated on with mention of one man who was supposed to have found the cave in which Walzer lived. But there is one sentence that sets it apart from all the rest. The story was published in the *Phoenix Gazette* in 1895.

"Robert McKee, a well to do prospector who has been all over the West, is in the city to gather data that will enable him to find the mythical mine once owned by Dutch Jacob, who in 1891 died in Phoenix. Mr. McKee is not a broke man, but an intelligent prospector that came to Arizona 2 years ago from Colorado. He once owned the tin mines near Rabbit, South Dakota, that have since been capitalized at $16,000,000. Since, in Arizona, he has hunted and prospected alternately, and in 2 years, 18 mountain lions have been captured, the result of his trapping, besides numerous bears. His outfit is a curiosity, consisting of 7 burros, one, an excellent saddle animal, a number of dogs, pure bred Shepards and Collies that are used in bear hunting,

several good guns, a very complete camping outfit, a well-filled purse and a fair bank account.

"Mr. McKee read in a recent Saturday Review, of a trip made into the Superstition Mountains by Frank Luke and Frank Kirkland, also about a former trip by P. C. Bickell. As the story goes, more than 30 years ago, two German prospectors were 56 miles SE of Phoenix, where they found 6 Mexicans working a rich gold mine. They were using the crude Spanish method, but were getting lots of gold. The Dutchman wanted the claim and took it by the easiest method, by killing the Mexicans. Dead men tell no tales.

"As civilization advanced Jacob and his partner became familiar with the people. Finally the partner disappeared probably by the same hand that dispatched the Mexicans.

"Finally the aged Jacob moved to the vicinity of Phoenix, but made frequent trips into the Superstition Mountains, each time bringing back with him bountiful supplies of gold. Old Jacob became a recluse and was later seen in Phoenix but once a year, just to vote the Republican ticket on election day. During the remainder of the time no one knew he was on the earth.

"He made his last trip in '84 and brought back $500.00 in two little sacks. He is now growing feeble. During his declining years a woman administered to the tottering Jacob as did Ruth in days of yore. To her he left his property, consisting of a town lot. He also divulged to her the secret of the hidden gold mine.

"In a gulch in the Superstition Mountains, the location of which is described by certain landmarks, there is a two room house in the mouth of a cave on the side of the slope near the gulch. Just across the gulch, about 200 yards, opposite this house in the cave, is a tunnel, well covered and concealed in the bushes. Here is the mine, the richest mine in the world, according to Dutch Jacob. Some distance above the tunnel on the side of the mountain, is a shaft or incline that is so steep that one cannot climb down. This, too, is carefully covered. The shaft goes right down in the midst of the rich gold ledge, where it can be picked off in flakes of almost pure gold.

"After Dutch Jacob had been buried the woman took a miner with her and spent an entire summer looking for the mine, but she was unable to find even the ruins of the house. She tried again the next year but failed, owing perhaps to the changes wrought by the heavy rains that annually fall in that section.

"Many had hunted for the mine even 20 years ago, and since the death of Dutch Jacob, J. E. Bark, P. C. Bickell, the journalist prospector, and many others have made frequent rips to that locality. In the fall of 1894 Bickell stumbled upon the stone house in the mouth of a cave. He felt as though he had obtained the secret but his grubstake was played out and he was compelled to seek civilization.

"With these facts, Mr. McKee proposes to go in a few days and make an intelligent search for the mine. He wishes to see the lady first and get a minute description of what she knows.

"The Dutch Jacob mine is a reality, and although it may not be found, it is highly probable that it will be. One thing is certain, the old man took great precautions to conceal the property which must be very rich, as he got the gold almost single-handed."

As mentioned before, this article, for the most part, is nothing more than another story of a man setting out to find the Lost Dutchman Mine that gives a brief account of one of the Dutchman legends. While it cannot be considered as absolute fact, there is one added bit of information given; a specific distance from Walzer's cave to the mine. Even though it is impossible to know if it is accurate, the second sentence in the sixth paragraph of the article should be duly noted. It reads, "Just across the gulch, about 200 yards, opposite this house in the cave, is a tunnel, well covered and concealed in the bushes."

While it is true that this is the only source thus far encountered that mentions a specific distance from the cave to the mine, another will be forthcoming and will be dealt with in detail. For now, a brief mention of it will suffice: On January 9, 1932, thirty-seven years after this article appeared in a Phoenix newspaper, the decapitated body of Adolph Ruth was found in the Superstition Mountains. In the decaying clothing on the body a notebook was found. At the bottom of one of the pages, following some instructions pertaining to the Lost Dutchman Mine which Ruth was seeking, hurriedly scribbled in Ruth's own handwriting were the words "Veni, Vidi, Vica . . . about 200 feet across from cave." And we all know that those Latin words mean I came, I saw, I conquered, but the important thing here is the distance mentioned: 200 feet . . . across from cave. The article stated that the mine was located 200 yards directly across from the cave.

Feet? Yards? Direct connection? Mere coincidence? I would not even hazard a guess, but it is remarkable.

This one last story regarding a cave in the Superstition Mountains has been reserved for last and separated from the others for a definite reason. For many, it will probably be as difficult to accept as was the story of the Mexican, Perez, and, when remembering the many false claims that have been made regarding the finding of gold in the Superstitions, this is very easy to understand. Nevertheless, this is no fake story. Nor is there the possibility of the details, such as they are, being in error. It is indeed unfortunate that the possibility and fear of legal entanglements has prevented the principals involved from making their discovery known to the public because they could have produced (and did to several men) actual and undeniable proof of their find.

There is a cave in the Superstitions in which a king's ransom in gold was found in the 1940's. This discovery was made by a party of six men. Upon this discovery, the men loaded all they could possibly carry into bags, and, after concealing the entrance to the cave as best they could, they left the mountains. This occurred shortly after WW II. During the following years, the men have made annual trips back to the cave to retrieve more gold. At the time of this writing only one of the men is still living and he now makes the trips alone. Naturally the location of this cave is a carefully guarded secret; it still contains a considerable amount of gold. The only information concerning the cave that can presently be divulged is the fact that it is shaped like an hour-glass, with one chamber above another.

There is not one shred of doubt in this writer's mind about the authenticity and accuracy of this report. Whether or not this cache was the source of Walzer's gold is not known. But, if not, Walzer sure missed a good one.

So go the stories of the discoveries of gold in the Superstitions. When you stop and look back, there has been quite a parade of individuals who have added fuel to the fire and have contributed to the legends. A parade that began well over a century ago and led by a small group of Mexican miners who dared to penetrate the unknown and were successful in finding the gold they were seeking but paid for the privilege with their lives. Next, there was the good Dr. Thorne whom the Apaches led into the mountains where they gave him a very unusual gift. Then there was Jacob Walzer, the Dutchman, who guarded his secret so well and, before his death, managed to take over a quarter-of-a-million dollars in gold from the Superstitions. Next in line were the two unfortunate soldiers and the equally unfortunate Joe Dearing, and on and on and on. The lure of the Superstitions is still as strong today as it was 50, 75, and even 100 years ago. The parade has not yet ended.

In the words of Horace, "Adhuc sub judice lis est." The case is still before the judge and has yet to be decided.

Chapter Ten

Silverlock
and Goldlock

The turn of the twentieth century found many changes in Arizona. Except for a few small renegade bands, the Indians were well under control. In 1906 the last of the great Apache warriors, Geronimo, died. Mineral wealth in the form of gold, silver, and copper was being taken from the earth in tremendous quantities. Arizona was beginning to come into its own. Finally, in 1912, it was accepted into the Union and became our 48th state.

However, the birth of this century found very few changes in the Superstition Mountains. There were a few ranches located in the very shadow of the mountains. Goldfield, with its Mammoth Mine belching gold, was experiencing its heyday. But in the heart of the Superstitions, there were no changes. The would-be finders of the Lost Dutchman Mine continued to come, but their search was in vain. The mountains still refused to give up their secrets.

It was in 1914 that two strange old men appeared on the scene and were responsible for this century's first big uproar concerning the gold of the Superstitions.

Known locally as Silverlock and Goldlock, their real names were C. H. Silverlocke and Malm (first name unknown). It was believed that they came to the area from Colorado, but, since they kept completely to themselves, no one seemed to know for sure. It was this anti-social and unfriendly attitude that prompted the local citizens to begin referring to them as "those two crazy men." And, to make matters worse, the two old men insisted in digging prospect holes on the western slope of the Superstition Mountain where everyone knew there was not the slightest trace of gold.

Crazy or not, they kept to themselves and continued digging their prospect holes. In spite of the natives' knowledge regarding that 'barren' western slope, they recovered over $15,000 in gold for their efforts.

The area where the two men worked was the site where the Apaches had massacred the Mexican miners so many years before. The gold they recovered was most likely a portion of the gold that had been lost during the battle. Unfortunately, Silverlock and Goldlock did not quit while they were ahead. After making their worthwhile find, they continued to search for still more gold until all their resources, including the gold they had found, were depleted. Eventually, Silverlock did lose his mind and was committed to a state institution for the insane. Malm, broke, old and alone, was sent to a county home for the aged. Both died a couple of years after their confinement.

There were many people who searched the Massacre Grounds after the old men were taken away, but if anyone was successful and found gold, they kept the fact to themselves.

While there can be very little doubt that the gold found there was the result of the massacre, it does not necessarily prove that its original source was in the Superstition Mountains. It could have been mined anywhere. However, the fact that it was found on a slope of the Superstition Mountains does open the door to the possibility that it was from the same source that Jacob Walzer obtained his gold, and what was found by Silverlock and Goldlock was merely what the Dutchman had left or failed to recover.

While there are many who refuse to accept this as a possible answer to the enigma of the Lost Dutchman Mine, it is, nevertheless, a possibility. If this is the case, thousands of people have searched for something that was found and exhausted over 50 years ago. It would indeed be ironic if the two old men, whom so many thought were unbalanced, had succeeded where others had failed and found the Lost Dutchman Mine. And, fate does have quite a reputation for the ironic.

It was also in the early years of this century that the Superstition Mountains began to receive national recognition for being something other than the location of the famed lost mine; they became known as the 'killer mountains' and one of the deadliest regions of the American Southwest.

Back in the early days of the West, to many death came quickly and violently. This was almost an accepted part of frontier life. So it was that for years men had met untimely deaths in the Superstitions, but it was not until this century that people began to wonder just who, or what, was responsible. This, too, is a question that has never been satisfactorily answered. And, now, as then, the mountains continue to take their toll.

In reviewing this facet of the history of the Superstitions, it is appalling, the number of people who have lost their lives in that relatively small area in the past 30 or 40 years. And, strangely, instead of the number decreasing, as you might think it would, sometimes it seems that it is actually increasing. At least this was true until a few years ago. A good portion of the deaths have been attributed to accidental or natural causes, but there have been numerous murders, and many of these cases are labeled "unsolved." Also included in the unsolved files are numerous attempted murders and several disappearances. There is no doubt that the Superstition Mountains came by their awesome reputation quite honestly.

Almost every student of the Lost Dutchman Mine has his own pet theories, or solutions, regarding these crimes. There are a few who actually believe the mountains are cursed, and the only thing waiting for those who dare seek the gold there is misfortune or death. Some individuals maintain that the Indians who are guarding a tribal treasure are responsible and kill anyone who gets too close to the place where it is hidden. There is another theory that is usually spoken only in whispers, but it has circulated for years and is by far the most terrifying to consider – – – According to some, a lone man with an insane obsession to keep the legend of the Lost Dutchman Mine alive has killed many people to make sure the mine was never found. He, they say, knows the location of the mine and, for years – – – decades – – – has guarded it. The suspected individual is dead now and this supposedly accounts for the lack of mysterious deaths in the mountains in recent years.

Most people, however, seem to believe that the killings that have occurred there can be attributed to various people who had various motives.

All these 'answers' are very intriguing, but, with one exception, they fall short when thinking objectively. In the first place, curses have no place in this modern world. They belong to an era of the past. It's most difficult to find anything supernatural about a bullet-hole in the back or between the eyes. And, this has been the cause of death in the majority of the unsolved murder cases. If the Indians, in attempting to guard a treasure, are responsible, they must have loot buried all over those mountains because unsolved murders, attempted murders, etc., have taken place in widely separated areas. Insofar as a mysterious Mr. X is concerned, this is a possibility, but there is nothing to prove it.

The least frightening and most easily acceptable theory is that no one party, or group, is responsible. Instead, that they are a series of crimes, that have no connection with each other. Of course, the Lost Dutchman Mine has been the motivating factor behind many of them, and in this sense, it could be said that some of them are connected. Regardless of who or why, any event involving foul play that occurs in the Superstition area automatically becomes a dark, mysterious matter with bizarre overtones until it is proven otherwise.

A perfect example of this occurred in 1964. A vacationing couple from New York were camping in the mountains and were found dead in their sleeping bags with their throats slashed. Immediately the rumors and talk began: the curse of the Dutchman's gold had taken another two victims!

It was a month or so later that the real flesh-and-blood villian was picked up by the police in another state while he was driving the camper truck he had stolen from the couple after murdering them. His motive was robbery, pure and simple, and had nothing whatsoever to do with the Lost Dutchman Mine. But, had the cards been stacked differently and he had not been caught, the chances are very good, that the deaths of the unfortunate couple would have been forever tagged as another example of the 'curse of the Superstitions'.

Similar situations are very likely the answer to many of the unsolved crimes the mountains are so famous for. Some – – – but not all! There have been some men who were killed solely because of what they knew about the Lost Dutchman Mine.

Along with the unsolved murders, there have been some that have been solved and were not at all mysterious. Some were the victims of old-fashioned gun battles. For a number of years, there was a feud going on between two groups who had claims in the Weavers Needle area. At least one death is known to have resulted from this feud.

And, there was the case of two young men who were very good friends and had joined forces to search for the Lost Dutchman Mine. Eventually, one wound up shooting the other and buried his body in a shallow grave.

There are two versions as to the motive for this crime. One, that the man who killed his friend did so because he suspected his partner of 'holding out' information. Another report states that after his capture, the young man said he was suddenly and inexplicably overcome with the urge to kill and, without even thinking, simply picked up his gun and shot his friend to death.

While there have been many murders, accidents are responsible for the majority of the deaths that have occurred in the Superstitions. And, the most unfortunate part of it all is that in many instances they could have been avoided if proper caution and planning had been exercised.

The frustration of searching for Walzer's gold has caused some suicides. Probably one of the first to choose death as a release from the obsession of finding the Lost Dutchman was Rhinehart Petrasch. As a young man, he was one of Jacob Walzer's friends. It was to him that Walzer revealed the key clues to the location of his mine. After the Dutchman died, Rhinehart sent for his brother and father to help him in his search for the mine. It was after his father, Peter Petrasch, that Peters Canyon was named; he reportedly spent most of his time searching in that particular canyon. Eventually, Rhinehart left Phoenix and later took his own life, supposedly because of his failure to find Walzer's mine.

While most of the accidents and deaths that have taken place in the Superstitions have been satisfactorily explained, there are those that have not, and it is these that are primarily responsible for the sinister reputation that hangs over the mountains like a shroud. Without a doubt, the most famous of all was the murder of Adolph Ruth.

Chapter Eleven

RUTH:
he came, he saw, ...?

Adolph Ruth was a crippled, retired government employee who went to Apache Junction in June of 1931 for the purpose of finding the Lost Dutchman Mine. To aid in his search, he had in his possession an old Spanish map that showed the location of a very rich gold mine located in the Superstition Mountains. The map had been given to his son, Erwin, by a prominent Mexican official. There was, and is, little doubt regarding its authenticity.

Ruth made two dire mistakes in his attempt to find the lost mine. First, he went into the mountains alone, and at one of the worst times of the year. But it was his second mistake that proved fatal; he told almost everyone who would listen that he had an authentic Peralta map.

After making local inquiry as to the location of a tall peak and being advised that it was most likely Weavers Needle, Ruth was packed into the mountains by a couple of local cowboys. They helped him set up camp near a permanent water hole in West Boulder Canyon and then left him alone to search for his El Dorado.

That was the end of Adolph Ruth. Six months later, in December, his skull, complete with bullet-hole was found by dogs on Black Top Mountain. The following month, his decapitated body was found in another area several miles away. Several items were found in the clothing on what was left of the body, but the map was not one of them. Nor was it found among his belongings at his camp. The map was gone.

One of the items found on the body was a small notebook. Information found in this notebook has perplexed would-be finders of the Lost Dutchman Mine for now over 40 years. In it, there was a passage written in Ruth's own handwriting, and, had not a portion of it been missing, there is a good possibility the puzzle of the source of the Dutchman's gold would have been solved years ago. But, regrettably, a portion of the memo was missing. The remainder of the message is very interesting, but confusing.

In essence, the words in the notebook implied that "it" was located within 2½ miles of Weavers Needle (no direction given) in a formation of basalt at approximately 2,500 feet elevation. The memo went on to state that there was a "monumented" trail located in the westernmost gorge on the south side of the mountain. It further stated that "they" followed this trail north and were led over a ridge and down past Sombrero Butte and into a canyon. From this point, they proceeded into a side canyon that was extremely dense with brush. At one time, there had been more to the message, but it was at this point that a portion of it had been destroyed. Further down on the page, as mentioned in a previous chapter, were the words "veni, vida, vica ...about 200 feet across from cave." These, too, in Ruth's handwriting.

While there is no way to know for sure, with the exception of the last notation, this was probably verbal information that Ruth had made note of to go along with the map. The final notation of Latin words is obvious; either Ruth or the party who originally supplied the information contained in the memo found whatever they had come to find 200 feet across from a cave.

The partially destroyed message can and has been interpreted to mean several different things, but nothing definite can be derived from it. But, the mention of 'it' (presumably the mine) being located in a formation of basaltic rock is interesting. Regardless of the fact that gold almost never occurs in this type of rock, this does coincide somewhat with other reports that have trickled out over the years.

In Sims Ely's book, *The Lost Dutchman Mine,* he tells of an aged Indian whom he interviewed once regarding the Lost Dutchman Mine. When asked the type of rock the gold was found in, the old Indian said it was dark, like the night. While one would be very foolish to believe everything they see in print, this writer has complete faith in the words of Mr. Ely, who was one of the most respected men in Arizona. There is the possibility, of course, that the old Indian was lying, but when considering the circumstances as related by Ely, this seems doubtful. The only question is whether or not the mine the Indian was referring to was the Lost Dutchman.

In conjunction with this, there are private, reliable reports stating that several black colored rocks extremely rich in gold have been found in the Superstition area a few miles west of the old silver mine workings north of Queen Creek. The rocks were found in an area where violent volcanic action had taken place and was very much in evidence.

In the case already mentioned involving the two Indians who made a trip into the Superstitions and came out and attempted to pay their motel bill with gold; the gold they presented was reportedly in a matrix comprised of basalt.

These reports span half a century, and are interesting but inconclusive. The matrix of the Dutchman's gold has been reported to be everything from three different types of quartz (pink, white, and bull) to hematitie, granite, and there are some who maintain that it was placer gold with no matrix at all. The type of ore is another thing that seems to change from one writer to another. Since no one has yet found the source of the Dutchman's gold, it is most difficult to understand how anyone could know for sure.

Of course, it is certainly within the realm of possibility, and maybe even likely, that there is more than one lost gold mine in the Superstition Mountains and this could easily account for the variations in the reports as to the type of ore involved. Naturally, any gold mine or deposit found in the Superstitions would be suspected of being the

Lost Dutchman, but, thus far, no one has found even one mine, much less two or more.

Another interesting aspect of the Adolph Ruth story is the map that disappeared when he was killed. It is common knowledge that he had the map on his person when he made his ill-fated journey into the mountains. Unless Ruth hid it in a still-unknown place, which seems doubtful under the circumstances, there is only one likely solution as to what happened to it; the killer took it. In fact, it is an accepted theory that he was murdered for the map, or that the killer watched and waited and killed Ruth after he actually found the mine and then took the map so no one else would get their hands on it.

Since Ruth's death, there have been several people who have claimed to be in possession of Ruth's map or a copy of it. This brings up a puzzling point: why these individuals, if one of them truly had the original map, would be so anxious to make it public knowledge. It would seem that since Ruth's killer was never caught, when and if the map he had with him ever turns up it would be at least an indirect link to the party responsible for his death. No doubt, the murderer has been dead for years, but, even so, it would be interesting to know how the party presently owning the map (if one exists) came into its possession. In fact, it would seem that law-enforcement officers would be most interested in this information since it should shed a certain amount of light on a still-unsolved crime. In any event, if the man who did murder Ruth took the map, as he apparently did, it is probably lost now for all time. If not, if the murderer did pass it on to someone else before he died, it is extremely doubtful that anyone who is now in possession of this map would make it known to anyone, and certainly not to newspapers.

Another famous unsolved and often written-about crime that has occurred in the Superstitions is the murder of James Cravey. While this chapter in the history of the mountains was not written until 16 years after Ruth's murder, the parallels of the two cases are remarkable.

Like Ruth, Cravey went into the mountains alone in search of the Lost Dutchman Mine. Also like Ruth, it was June when he went into the mountains. But instead of being packed in on horses, Cravey and his supplies were taken in by helicopter. He was set down near the head of La Barge Canyon where he made his camp. And, as in the Ruth case, this was the last time he was ever seen alive. Cravey also shared a disability similar to Ruth's; he was crippled. The time lapse between the time the two men went into the mountains and when their bodies were found is very close. Cravey's body was found seven months after he disappeared; Ruth's body was found six months after he went into the Superstitions. *Both men had been beheaded.*

It was in the latter part of February, 1948, that Cravey's body was found under very bizarre circumstances. Two men who were out hiking came upon a rope stretched across the trail in front of them. One end of the rope led into the dense brush at the side of the trail. Upon investigation, they found the grisley bundle; a headless body wrapped in a blanket and bound with one end of the rope. Nearby on a boulder, they found a jacket, and in the pockets was a wallet that still contained money and identification papers bearing the name of James Cravey.

But the most intriguing aspect of all is the location where the body was found – – – and, how it was found. It was a full seven months from the time Cravey disappeared until his body was found. The trail that the rope was stretched across was well-traveled and, without a doubt, many people had hiked up and down it during the seven month period. And Cravey had been dead for months when his body was found. It would have been all but impossible that someone would not have noticed the rope had it been there for any period of time at all. It would seem that someone must have placed the body there and rigged the rope across the trail not too long before it was found. Certainly not more than a matter of weeks. But, the question is why anyone would resort to such tactics.

Perhaps someone simply found the body in a remote area and wanted to turn it over to the authorities but did not want to get involved. However, this certainly is not how most people would have handled it if they discovered a headless corpse in the wilderness. The only other explanation is that it was placed there by the killer; perhaps so that the search for Cravey would come to an end and stop people from poking around the area. In any event, his skull was found a few days later, and the remains were later definitely identified as Cravey.

While Cravey did not have a map, it was known that he had pertinent information concerning the Lost Dutchman Mine. In fact, it was believed that he knew almost the exact location. Nor was it his first trip into the mountains. He had already made one trip in on foot and had determined that it would be impossible for him to get enough pack animals with adequate supplies into the area he had pinpointed. Therefore, he had chartered the helicopter to fly him and his supplies in. Apparently someone believed he was on a hot trail, followed him, and killed him.

There have been many other unsolved murders in the Superstitions, but the fact that both Cravey and Ruth were beheaded does give an especially sinister note to these two cases. While there is nothing definite to connect them, the similarities and coincidences between the two are certainly very interesting.

As recently as the 1960's, bodies of individuals seeking the Lost Dutchman Mine were still being found. During the years from 1951 to 1961, twelve people met an untimely death and two completely disappeared in the Superstition Mountains. Of the twelve, one death was attributed to suicide; another was the result of a gun battle and was termed self-defense. Another man was killed when he attacked a couple that was hiking in the mountains, and was shot in a struggle for a gun. There was a young girl who apparently was killed in a fall from a cliff, and still another individual was killed by his partner. The remaining seven people were shot and killed by parties unknown.

One unusual aspect of these deaths is that of the seven victims, five of the bodies were found in the months of February or June. It was in June that Ruth and Cravey disappeared, and in February that Cravey's body was found. Of the five solved deaths, only one took place in either of these months.

It would be most difficult to try and ascertain just what this means, if anything, but it does tax the mind when trying to accept it all as mere coincidence. It almost makes one wonder if perhaps there is not something to the whispered rumor of the insane man who murdered to keep the legend of the lost mine alive. In any event, it would seem that June and February are bad months for trips into the Superstitions.

Chapter Twelve

"We found it!"
"We found..."
"We..."

Closely akin to the claims made by those who maintain they have an original Peralta map, but by far more numerous, are the reports made by various individuals stating they have found the Lost Dutchman Mine. No need to point out that almost all of these claims must be taken with a grain of salt, if, indeed, not all of them. It takes nothing more than a minimum of common sense to see through most of these publicized claims. For example, an article appeared in the December 19, 1965 edition of the *ARIZONA REPUBLICAN*, a Phoenix newspaper, concerning a man who maintained that he owned the Peralta map.

Not only does he state that he owns the map, but says that he found a cache of bullion worth over two billion dollars. A few sentences later, he mentions that he also located two veins of gold and estimated that it would take ten years to recover it. It's needless to point out that a cache of bullion and veins of gold are two entirely different things. Are we to believe that he found both? In another paragraph he states that he found a pair of spurs at the site and says that he was offered over $150,000 for them, but turned down the offer. On the other hand, he says that he had to raise money to finance the operation from individuals in the East.

While this story is within the realm of possibility, it is a 'little' difficult to believe, and since seven years has passed since this article appeared, one can't help but wonder why there has been no further announcements regarding this discovery.

Almost every year at least one person makes a public announcement to the effect that they have found the Lost Dutchman Mine, and their evident inability to produce any evidence whatsoever to back up their claim does not seem to discourage them in the least. Without a doubt, the legendary mine has been found over fifty times, and, invariably, in almost as many different places.

Various accounts of one report which may someday prove to be more worthwhile appeared in many newspapers throughout the country in April of 1966. It concerns a group of men from one of the mid-western states who, according to their spokesman, found the Lost Dutchman Mine. An article that appeared in a Phoenix newspaper states that papers filed with the county recorder's office indicates that the mine is located "somewhere within 1,200 acres in the Bluff Springs Mountain area."

This is another report where the Ruth, or Peralta, map enters into the picture. According to their spokesman, the mine was found by using a map, or maps, that had been obtained from one of Adolph Ruth's sons. At the time this article was published, it was reported that the maps were locked in a safety deposit box. In 1968, they were published in a book titled THE KILLER MOUNTAINS by Curt Gentry.

Some of the information given out by the group's spokesman at the time was somewhat confusing. For example, he reportedly stated that the mine was located exactly where the Dutchman said it was, and that every clue Walzer left checked out and was correct. I am sure that everyone who has ever seriously researched the Lost Dutchman Mine, and spent hour upon hour and year after year studying the well-known clues and trying to make them coincide with the terrain, landmarks, and features of the mountains would be most interested in knowing just what clues the gentleman was referring to; surely not the ones that are so well known. One member of the group reportedly stated that Walzer was killed by Indians; records show that he died in Phoenix of natural causes. Another puzzling aspect of this story is that the group said the mines were originally owned by the Catholic Church, and that it was from old Church records that the Peraltas obtained information that enabled them to find them. If the Catholic Church ever owned gold mines in the Superstition Mountains, it would be interesting to know where records to this effect can be found.

Nevertheless, the leader of this group did evidently contact an Erwin Ruth, who was reported to be the son of Adolph Ruth, and obtained a tracing of the copy of the map Ruth took into the mountains with him. And, it has been rumored for years that Ruth did leave a copy of the map with his family.

According to the book THE KILLER MOUNTAINS, what the group originally found and thought was the Lost Dutchman Mine turned out not to be the genuine article, but, apparently, at the time the book was written, the group still felt sure that it was merely a matter of time before they did find the mine.

One interesting aspect of the maps that appeared in the book is the fact that the leader of the group believes that the main map has to be held up and viewed in a mirror in order for the landmarks to appear in their proper place. In other words, according to the book, the Peraltas drew the map with everything reversed. This could very well be true, but there is an area about 5½ miles north of Weavers Needle that bears a striking resemblance to most of the features shown on the map, as is.

But the fact remains, no known gold production has come from the Superstitions at the time of this writing. And, when and if a rich deposit of gold is found in the Superstition Mountains it will, in time, become public knowledge and there will be no doubt about it. It will be mined as any other profitable gold deposit is mined. Since a large portion of the Superstition area is within a National Wilderness area and a National Forest, permission from the United States government would be necessary before any mining could be carried on there, and it would soon become a cut-and-dried situation. In fact, in the very near future, it may be impossible to continue even prospecting in the Superstitions due to new laws that are now in the works.

On the other hand, a small group could locate a rich gold deposit and profitably work it on a small scale and secretly. But needless to say, no one will ever hear about it.

Chapter Thirteen

The Signs of
EL DORADO

Since time immemorial, man has found it necessary, on occasion and for one reason or another, to bury or conceal his most valuable possessions. There is little reason to believe this practice will ever cease.

While it is not as prevalent as many people seem to believe, some individuals do draw waybills, or maps, or mark the site where they have secreted their valuables. Some treasures have been recovered over the years through the proper interpretation of such maps and markings. But, most of the so-called treasure maps and markings have only baffled the treasure hunter, and, in spite of thorough study and search, very rarely do they lead to a successful recovery of treasure.

This is not necessarily because the treasure is nonexistent or has already been found, but because the map, or markings, have not been correctly understood. The reason for this is simply because they were not meant to be understood – – – at least by anyone other than the person who drew them or the party for which they were intended.

There are numerous so-called treasure signs that are considered to be universal. But, many of these often have two or more possible meanings and there is always the possibility they had still another meaning to the person who used them. A perfect example of this is the simple cross. It, of course, has been and is used to mark graves, but it has also been used, supposedly, to indicate the location of treasure. And, to confuse the issue even further, the padres of long-ago would often times carve crosses into trees and boulders as trail markers. Other cross-like markings have proved to be nothing more than 'doodlings' made by the Indians.

Though there are a few exceptions, ordinarily before you can hope to successfully translate treasure signs, maps, or waybills, it is necessary to know something about the personality, or character, of the person who made them. Often times, knowing something of what the treasure consists of will help. Without some advanced knowledge of the circumstances and situation, it is almost hopeless. For example, should I ever conceal a treasure and draw a map showing its location, I would very likely use the numeral '17'. Anyone who ever tried to decipher the map would invariably interpret the 17 as the amount or number of something, or perhaps, decide that it signified the 17th letter of the alphabet, when, actually, the numeral would connote something else entirely to me under those circumstances. So it is with most of the coded documents and maps concerning the location of buried or hidden treasure.

However, there have been instances when signs and symbols and maps have paved the way for successful and fruitful treasure hunts. And, there is nothing quite as challenging as knowing that you have an authentic waybill to a treasure and realizing the only thing necessary for success is being able to figure it out. This is a true battle of wits. But, unfortunately, all too often, the would-be trover is the loser, and, though usually dead for years, the man who concealed the treasure is the victor.

Near the junction of Charlesbois and La Barge Canyons in the Superstition Mountains there is a huge boulder known as Petroglyph Rock. Carved into this boulder are numerous signs, symbols and other markings. Some people maintain that they were carved by the Peraltas and believe that in these strange markings lie the secret to a fabulous gold mine.

But not all of the 'treasure signs' that exist in the Superstitions are confined to this one boulder. Others have been found in various places, from the southern foothills to the northern-most perimeter of the area, but these are usually comprised of only one or two symbols in any one place. There is one exception to this: on the southern side of the Superstition Mountain, proper, there is a canyon that cuts into the mountain and is known as Hieroglyphic Canyon. There, picture writings carved into the rocks exist in great profusion. But it is now known that these markings are definitely of Indian origin and are not Spanish treasure signs.

The markings that appear on Petroglyph Rock have puzzled would-be finders of the Lost Dutchman Mine for years. While many people believe they have them properly interpreted, they have been unable to follow their translations to a successful end. While these signs and symbols could be connected with Spanish mining activities in the area as many believe, there is considerable room for doubt that this is true. Nevertheless, they do justify consideration.

As you will note in Illustration A, the predominant marking on Petroglyph Rock is a crude figure resembling a man with a large head and a triangular-shaped body. This figure appears to be carrying a bag on his back. Directly in front of him is what resembles a shepherd's staff. Left of this staff and extending over into the middle of the picture, there is a series of circles, some with dots in the middle. Many of these circles are joined together by connecting lines. Near the bottom of the staff there is a small figure resembling a 'Q', but instead of the tail of the Q being curved, it is comprised of right angles. Further to the left and beside the series of circles, there is a coiled figure, looking very much like a snake with half the body coiled and the other half extending downward. While there are many other markings, these are the most dominant.

Most of the individuals who have made their interpretations of these markings public maintain that the man-like figure represents a miner carrying an ore sack on his back. And, when viewed as one figure, it does take on this appearance. However, when studying it closely, it

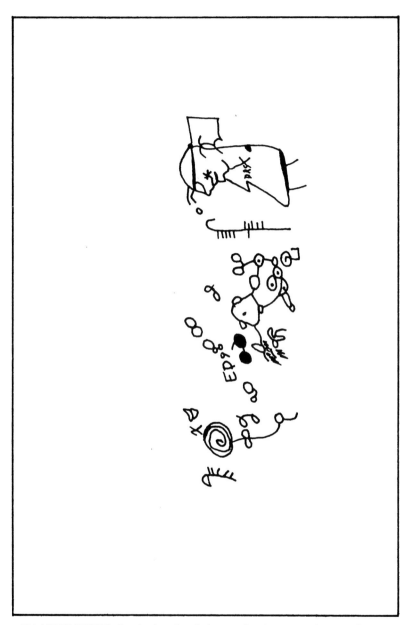

ILLUSTRATION A: A sketch of the predominant carvings on Petro-glyph Rock.

can be broken down into several individual symbols. Beginning with the vertical line that forms the 'back' of the man and then following it up towards the head, close scrutiny will reveal that the markings forming the ear, the dot at the back of the head, and a portion of the bag form the figure of a turtle — a well-known treasure sign that usually indicates a direction. On the face, halfway between the ear and the nose, is what appears to be a six-pointed star, a symbol that can have several meanings. The lines in the mid-section of this man-like figure cross to form an 'X', and beside it, in extremely small characters, is what appears to be the word 'oro', which we all know is the Spanish word for gold.

Insofar as the marking that resembles a staff is concerned, it looks like very little other than that. However, there are small horizontal lines extending out from it, and, using a great deal of imagination, it could possibly represent a ladder.

The next figure to be considered is the Q-like character near the bottom of the staff. There is a sign that resembles this that has been used for centuries, but instead of a circle, the body of the symbol is a square, and it represents one and a half quadrants, or 135°. There is also a sign that is somewhat similar that represents a spring of water.

The series of circles appears to be completely without rhyme or reason, but there are some who believe they represent the mines. How they came to this conclusion is anyone's guess.

The coiled figure does have the appearance of a snake, but it could also pass for the capital letter 'P', as used in the 1700's, as well as a half dozen other things. Incidentally, the snake is often times found in what are believed to be treasure signs. But, the snake is fundamentally a religious sign.

Perhaps there are some individuals who are clever enough to find definite meanings in these markings, put them together, and come up with a message, but this writer has been unable to do so. While a message of a sort can be derived from the man-like figure when it is broken up into several individual symbols, this is but a portion of the message (if there is one), and even if the translation is correct, it would be useless without being able to translate the balance of the markings.

While the possibility exists that these are Spanish treasure signs as many suspect, it is more probable that they are of Indian origin, and, most likely, ancient Indian.

Some of the figures are very similar to those used by the Toltec and Aztec Indians in Mexico. In some ways, the man-like figure resembles crude carvings that have been found of the ancient Aztec god of learning, Quetzalcoatl. And there is much speculation in some circles regarding a possible connection between the Hohokams, who are known to have inhabited the area, and the Aztecs. In any event, it could be a crude likeness of this very important god. Or, it could well be nothing more than a carving of an Indian carrying a burden of some sort. Also, it could be simply geographic or climatic signs along an old trail.

AIR&SPACE
Smithsonian

SAVINGS CERTIFICATE

Return this card to enjoy the privileges of membership in the National Air & Space Museum, and you'll get exciting issues of **AIR & SPACE** magazine too!

☐ 14 issues only $49 · **SAVE 41%**
☐ 7 issues only $29 · **SAVE 30%**

Name: _____
                 (Please Print)

Address: _____

City: _____ State: ____ Zip: _____

E-mail Address: Please send me email updates from Air & Space magazine.

☐ Payment enclosed.   ☐ Please bill me later.

ASYDD54

Air & Space is published seven times a year, but may occasionally publish special issues. Savings are off the $5.99 per issue newsstand price. Please add $6 per year for foreign orders and prepay in U.S. funds. Ninety-nine percent of dues is allocated for magazine subscription. Please allow 4-6 weeks to receive your first issue.

As with almost everything else pertaining to the Lost Dutchman Mine, there can be no definite conclusions reached regarding the signs and symbols on Petroglyph Rock. Several authorities in the field of cryptology have examined them and cannot agree as to their origin or meaning. Spanish treasure signs or Indian picture writings? No one seems to know.

However, some of the other 'treasure signs' to be found in the Superstition area are definitely of Spanish origin, and while it is not difficult to translate them using the usual meanings, none of them, to date, has led anyone to the famed lost mine.

A new wrinkle was added to the enigma of the Lost Dutchman Mine in June of 1964 when an article titled "Mysterious Maps To Lost Gold Mines" appeared in *LIFE* magazine. This article was devoted to three intricately carved stone tablets that were allegedly found in the southern foothills of the Superstition Mountains in the 1950's. A brief account is given concerning the efforts of the man who found them to translate them and put his translations to use. The article then goes on to tell how the tablets fell into the hands of an individual known as Travis Marlowe. Included with the article are excellent photographs showing two of the tablets and a portion of the third, but some of the markings were covered by tape and were not visible in the photographs.

In January of 1965, a small booklet written and published by Marlowe was released. Titled *Superstition Treasures,* it primarily deals with the author's version of the Peralta-Dutchman story, his interpretation of portions of the tablets, and his efforts to locate 18 gold mines in the Superstition Mountains, the exact location of which he believes is revealed by the tablets. Excellent photographs are included, but, as in the article, some of the markings are blacked out and not visible. Since then photos may have appeared in other publications as well, but excellent drawings of the tablets showing all the markings appeared in Volume 3/Number 1 issue of *The Treasure Hunter,* edited and published by Johnny Pounds at Midway City, California. The tablets are reportedly now in an Arizona museum.

The first thing to be considered is the authenticity of the tablets. In the Foreword of the Marlowe book, there is a statement to the effect that the tablets were examined by a professor of geology at one of the state universities who declared them to be genuine and carved approximately 100 years ago. Unfortunately, neither the name of the professor or the university is given making it impossible to verify this statement, but, since the tablets have been accepted by a museum, there is very little, if any, reason to doubt their authenticity. In fact, there are reasons to believe they may have been carved much more than a century ago.

The second point for consideration is the allegation that the tablets were found in the southern foothills of the Supersitions. There is no way the researcher can verify this, but there is no reason whatsoever to believe they were found elsewhere. Nevertheless, granting that they were found in the Superstition area does not necessarily prove that they were buried there intentionally. Nor does it prove that they actually pertain to the Superstition area. It is possible that the tablets came to be there quite by accident; perhaps lost from the back of a pack mule or abandoned there by a party who suffered some sort of misfortune, and over the years were naturally covered by the never-ceasing shuffling sand.

The third question is whether or not the tablets actually pertain to material treasure in any form. Ordinarily, when it comes to so-called treasure maps, there is a story surrounding them. And, regardless of the extent of truth to these tales, most of them offer an answer of a sort to the questions of what the treasure consists of, who buried or concealed it, and why. Of course, these stories cannot be depended on until they have been thoroughly checked out, but the researcher at least has the advantage of being able to study and investigate the situation, and make some sort of determination about it. This is not so in the case of the stone tablets. Not only is the what, who, and why a complete mystery, but there is actually nothing substantial indicating that they involve treasure at all. It goes without saying that the tablets were carved for a precise purpose, but, when being completely objective, just what this purpose was remains to be seen.

Nevertheless, treasure hunting history has proven that this type of stone sculpture, such as the famed Spider Rock of Oklahoma, has led to buried treasure. Therefore, the belief that the stone tablets were carved to show the location of treasure, in one form or another, is not at all far-fetched. And, since they were found in the Superstition area and there is nothing proving anything to the contrary, it is reasonable to assume that they do pertain to that area.

Unlike the signs and symbols cut into Petroglyph Rock, those carved into the stone tablets were meticulously cut and are true works of art. All three of the tablets are about the same size and weigh about 25 pounds each. On one of them there is a figure dressed in flowing robes, and apparently represents a saint or padre. This figure is holding a cross. Beneath the cross there is a series of small characters including the numerals 1, 2, 3, 4, and 8. Boldly carved and to the right are the words "ESTA BEREDA ES PELIGROZA – YO BOY 18 LUGARES – BUSCA EL MAPA – BUSCA EL COAZON." Faintly and at the extreme right edge of the tablet are the words "SONORA MEX."

Some of the words carved into this tablet are misspelled, but they have been translated to mean "This Trail Is Dangerous. I Go 18 Places. Study The Map. Study The Heart." This does, indeed, seem to be the message, but there are some indications that this could be a coded message with hidden and underlying meanings.

The one outstanding feature of these letters, or words, is the fact that in the word 'peligroza', the last eight letters are only about one-half the size of the other letters. The reason for this could be because the individual who carved them did not allow enough room and found it necessary to reduce the size of these letters in order to economize on space. But, when considering the workmanship and

Tablet 1   Tablet 2   Tablet 3

ILLUSTRATION B: Drawings showing principal markings on stone tablets.

perfection involved, this seems somewhat doubtful. Instead, there could be a deliberate reason why these letters are smaller.

The next thing to consider is the misspelled words. There is no such word in the Spanish language as 'bereda'. The Spanish word for trail, which is what this word had been translated to mean, is 'vereda'. Here, either in error or intentionally, the letter V was replaced with a B. The word 'peligroza' is also spelled incorrectly. The correct spelling for the word which means dangerous is 'peligrosa'; the incorrect letter being a Z. The word 'boy' is also misspelled. In the translation, it is believed that the word intended was 'voy', meaning 'I go'. Again, a B was used instead of the correct letter V. The final misspelled word on this tablet is 'coazon'. The correct spelling for the word meaning heart is 'corazon'; an R was omitted.

While not being misspelled, the word 'busca' has been misused. Busca is a noun meaning "a search, or an examination." If a verb meaning "you search or you examine" is what was intended, the word should have been 'buscar'. If so, as in the word 'coazon', an R has been omitted.

Whether there is any significance whatsoever to the incorrect letters that were used or the correct ones that should have been used is anyone's guess, but, most likely, they are merely the result of poor spelling.

On the reverse side of the tablet depicting the saint, there is an excellent likeness of a horse, along with various other symbols including markings that appear to indicate a river, creek, or, perhaps, the outline of a range of mountains. There is another curved line that evidently does represent a river as the word 'Rio' appears directly beneath it. On the left side of the tablet are the words "EL COBOLLO DE SANTA FE." Here, again, is a misspelled word. The word for horse which is what was apparently intended is 'coballo'; an O was used instead of the correct letter A. Translated, these words simply mean "The Horse Of Santa Fe". On the right side of this tablet are the words "YO PASTO – AL NORTE – DEL RIO." Loosely translated, this means "I Pasture To The North By The River," and, apparently, these words are being spoken by the horse since only a horse, or some other four-footed animal, 'pastures'. Needless to say that no one is going to carve stone tablets showing the location of where a horse pastures, so it is safe to assume that the horse represents something other than a horse, and, if the tablets do pertain to a treasure, it seems reasonable to consider the possibility that the horse represents the treasure. If so, then the words "El Coballo De Santa Fe" would actually mean that the treasure was from Santa Fe, and the words "Yo Pasto Al Norte Del Rio" would mean that it is located to the north by (or near) a river. And, when remembering the saint on the reverse side of the tablet, it appears that it would be a Church treasure.

Before going on to discuss the other tablets, it might be well to point out that on the side of the tablet portraying the saint, the numbers near the cross the figure is holding, when added together total 18.

The two remaining tablets are all but impossible to describe as there are very few identifiable characters and figures present. The most predominant feature of the second tablet is a curved line into which ten holes, approximately the same distance apart, have been carved. There is also a wavy line that extends completely across the tablet, as well as several numerals and other markings. On the opposite side of this tablet, in very large letters, is the word "DON."

The third and final tablet appears to be a continuation of the second tablet, or, perhaps, a specific portion of the second tablet greatly enlarged. At the top of this tablet, deeply carved, is a horizontal curved line extending from one side of the tablet to the other. In the center of the tablet is a large recessed heart. In the bottom of this heart-shaped recessed area are the numerals *1 8 4 7*. While this seems to be a date, it is difficult to understand why anyone would make such a production out of dating the tablets. This opens the door to the possibility that the numbers signify something else. Incidently, these numerals also appear on the tablet bearing the figure of a saint or padre.

Another very predominant figure on the third tablet is a dagger. Leading up from the bottom of the tablet and extending to the heart-shaped area, there is a curved line with four holes, or dots, carved into it. There is a large cross carved into the reverse side of this tablet.

A small heart-shaped stone which fits into the recessed heart on the third tablet was reportedly found, but the only photographs that have appeared of this small stone show only small oval-shaped markings.

It seems that the most popular theory regarding these tablets is that they were carved by Pedro Peralta in the late 1840's, and show the location of 18 gold mines in the Supersition Mountains. At least one individual believes that he has found markers in the mountains and southern foothills that correspond with many of the symbols on the tablets. While the 'markers' that have been found could correlate with the tablets, some of the reports regarding them and how this conclusion was reached seems a little far-fetched.

It is somewhat difficult to understand how the conclusion was reached that there are 18 gold mines involved. The only word on the tablets connected with the number 18 is the word 'lugares'. This word means nothing more than places, or sites; the Spanish word for mines is 'mina'. Without a doubt, the numeral 18 is very important in the message of the tablets, and it is also apparent that something involved numbers 18. It is possible that the word 'lugares' means something other than the places, or sites, but why not 18 leagues, 18 camps, 18 markers, or 18 of almost anything else. What was used as a basis for the conclusion that there are 18 mines? Once you have strayed from the correct translation, though it is most difficult to understand why anyone would, almost anything can be substituted.

Several scars, holes, and other markings that have been found in saguaro cactus in the area are believed by some to be treasure signs and symbols connected with the stone tablets. There are several things to be considered here.

While my knowledge regarding botany leaves much to desired, it is my understanding that the rate of growth for the saguaro is very spasmodic. It takes something like three years for it to grow from a seed into a plant a few inches high. By the time the saguaro is 30 years old it is all of three feet high, more or less. It takes another 70 years, or 100 years, in all, for it to reach its maximum height. This, of course, is generally speaking; some will grow a little faster and others, a little slower, depending on rainfall, temperatures, etc. After reaching full maturity, and under good conditions, it will live another 100 to 150 years, making its full life span approximately 200 to 250 years.

Some of the markings that are believed to be treasure signs made by the Peraltas are said to be cut into the saguaros at man's height, or about 6 feet. A symbol or marking cut into a saguaro 120 years ago six feet above the ground could, at this time, still be only six feet above the ground, but only if the saguaro was fully grown at the time the symbol was cut. Otherwise, the cactus would have grown since then and the marking would be somewhat higher. It is very possible that our feathered friend, the woodpecker, who is notorious for pecking holes and nesting in the saguaro, is responsible for a good many of these 'treasure signs'.

Before leaving the subject of saguaros and their connection (if any) to the alleged gold of the Supersitions there is something else that should be pointed out. Considerable emphasis has been placed by some individuals on series of saguaros that have grown to form a straight line. These are thought by many to have been planted by man, presumably the Peraltas, in such a fashion to act as a treasure marker. In fact, this writer has found a group of seven giant saguaros growing in just such a fashion on the side of a mountain a mile or so east of Tortilla Mountain. They could not possibly have formed a straighter line had they been planted by someone using a gigantic straight-edge. It is very easy to understand why someone might believe they were planted. Of course, it is possible that they were but there are sound reasons for doubt.

According to available information, the young saguaro seedling has a very slim chance of surviving. Of the millions of seeds that are dispersed by a mature plant, the chances are poor that any of them will take root and grow. For survival, the seed must come to rest in a place that is protected from the sun before it can take root and grow. The young seedling must have shade and cannot be exposed to full sun. The only ones that stand much chance of making it are the seeds that come to rest under the protective branches of scrub brush or another protective plant.

Due to the weight of the saguaro (even those a few feet in height weigh hundreds of pounds and a fully grown plant weighs many tons), it would have been very difficult for anyone a hundred or so years ago to transplant a well-started 30 or 40 year old saguaro. While they are rugged looking giants, these plants are very delicate while maturing. Even today, with controlled temperatures, etc., horticulturists find the saguaro a very difficult plant to grow. It seems highly improbable that the Mexicans would have been successful in growing them like a row of corn. This, plus the fact that there are several places in the Superstition area where these 'rows' of saguaros exist tend to make it extremely doubtful that they have any significance insofar as a treasure or gold mines are concerned.

Needless to say, there are many ways to approach the problem of interpreting the stone tablets. And, using a maximum amount of both imagination and hypothesis, just as many possible interpretations. Probable interpretations are another matter entirely. But regardless of how far-fetched or sound any one particular interpretation may seem, its validity can be neither proved nor disproved until and unless treasure of some sort is actually found. As with all other so-called treasure maps and waybills, there is an old adage that was never more applicable: The proof of the pudding lies in the eating!

Even though it may be nothing more than coincidence, there are a couple of other famed lost treasures the information about which corresponds more closely with the markings on the stone tablets than does the known information concerning the alleged Peralta mines.

One of these treasures is believed to be hidden or buried in the Coballo Mountains of New Mexico. These mountains are located along the infamous Jornada del Muerte (Journey of Death) which was the route used by the Spaniards to traverse the distance between El Paso and the pueblo of Santa Fe. Just as the name implies, this trail penetrated a waterless wasteland that was plagued by maurauding Indians, murderous bandits, and the never-relenting sun. It was truly a journey of death for many (Esta Bereda Es Peligroza — this trail is dangerous).

While there are several treasures believed to be buried in or near the Coballo Mountains, the story that will be presented here concerns one that is allegedly hidden or buried near an old Spanish water hole at the southwest corner of the mountains and involves a Mexican named Pedro Navarez.

Navarez was a peon turned soldier who accompanied the Spanish army on many of their expeditions and undertakings into the area which is now New Mexico. The enlisted men's lot was a rough one; they were forced to suffer many abuses at the hands of their superiors. Finally, Pedro had all he could take and in 1639, he deserted.

After being accepted by the Apaches he adopted their way of life and lived with them for the following ten years. And, when he accepted their way of life, he went all the way. Often times he accompanied the Indians on their raids that were carried out against the Spaniards as they were transporting gold, silver, and supplies to and from Mexico. Afterward, they would take the loot and conceal or bury it in the Coballos.

Things went well for Navarez until he was finally captured in 1649 and returned to Mexico for trial. After being tried and convicted for treason, he was sentenced to death. Facing execution, he wanted to make his confession for the absolution of his soul, and chose to do so in writing. And, as was decreed by the court, on the appointed day, Navarez was taken from his cell and hanged.

It was many years before the confession Navarez had written was found in the midst of many other old church records. Included in this confession was a waybill concerning a tremendous amount of gold and silver that was hidden in a range of mountains that could be none other than the Coballo Mountains of New Mexico.

The waybill can be found in its entirety in Jesse Ed Rascoe's book, *The Golden Crescent.* Only portions of it will be discussed here.

The first passage that is relative here mentions a large stone with a cross, a small plot of ground 100 yards below, a small stone, and 18 "atajos." It is interesting at this point to remember the figure of the saint on the first stone tablet. The saint is holding a cross. Beneath the cross there is a small heart-shaped figure that could represent the small heart-shaped stone that was reportedly found with the stone tablets. Also beneath the cross are numerals which total 18. And, of course, there is a large cross on the backside of the third tablet.

To my knowledge, no one has been able to translate the word 'atajos', but, whatever it means, there are 18 of them involved with the Navarez treasure, just as there are 18 lugares involved with the stone tablets.

Reference is made in the Navarez waybill to three caves, one much larger than the other two, and containing a quantity of silver bars, tools, and other objects. These caves are said to be located in an area near a stream and some small tombs. The numeral 3 appears repeatedly on the stone tablets; on the side of the tablet depicting a horse there are three circles with dots in the center that could represent caves, a wavy horizontal line that could represent a stream, and, directly beneath it, there are crosses that could represent tombs.

So, here we have a treasure that is concealed in the Coballo Mountains, an area that at the time could only be reached by an extremely dangerous trail. A trail that led to and from Santa Fe. The principal involved is named Pedro, and there is a large stone with a cross on it and 18 'atajos' involved.

Actually, it is very doubtful that the stone tablets are in any way connected with the Navarez treasure. These particulars have been presented solely to point out that there are other treasure stories where the information comes much closer to tying in with the markings on the tablets than do the stories surrounding lost gold mines in the Superstition Mountains. It is fairly safe to assume that had the tablets been found elsewhere, no one would have ever connected them with the Superstitions. And, it should be remembered that there is no way of knowing if the tablets were buried where they were found or if they came to be there by accident.

After studying the markings and words on the tablets very carefully and doing considerable research on the Spanish era of our Southwest, it seems quite possible that instead of 18 gold mines in the

Superstitions, the Tablets, when interpreted correctly, might reveal pertinent information concerning the location of several large treasure caches buried or hidden in various places along the route between Santa Fe and El Paso — treasure that was hidden long before the mid-1800's.

This is not to say that there are not similarities between the markings on the tablets and the features and topography of the Supersititon area because there most assuredly are.

Without a doubt, there are many meanings that can be found in the tablets if one uses his imagination and studies them carefully. But, there are simply too many and's, if's, and but's involved to make safe any one conclusion. There is a theory that there are other tablets that remain to be found. If so, when and if they are found, perhaps they will shed further light on a now very cloudy situation. Regardless, the stone tablets do exist and have added another page to the ever-growing legend of the Superstition Mountains. And, who knows? Perhpas they do hold the secret to the legendary riches of the mountains.

COINCIDENCE?

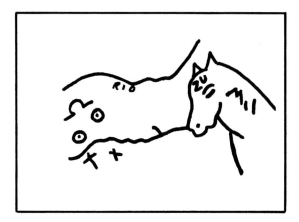

ILLUSTRATION C: The upperleft section of the stone tablet depicting the horse. Note the 'rio' marked line.

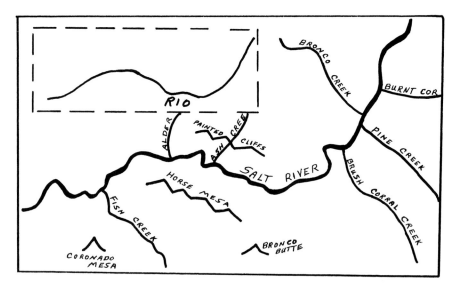

ILLUSTRATION D: Enlarged sketch of a section of the Salt River that is similar to the 'rio' marked line (see inset).

ILLUSTRATION E: Sketch of the second and third stone tablets combined (see illustration F).

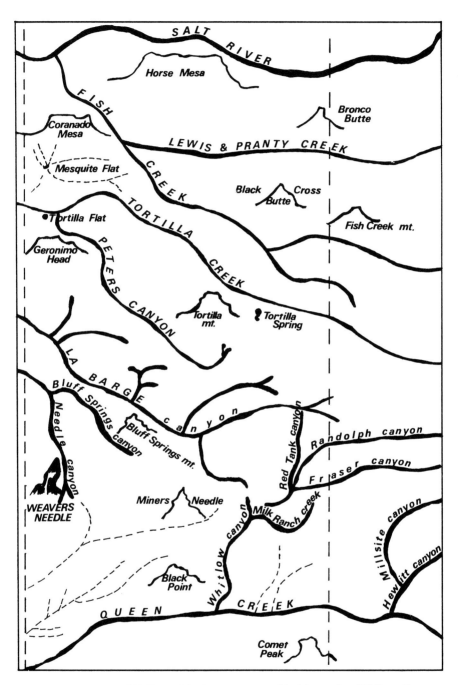

ILLUSTRATION F: Is this the area covered in Illustration E? Note the curvatures of the Salt River and Queen Creek.

80

Chapter Fourteen

FOUND?

My first glimpse of the Superstition Mountains came in the early 1960's and, strangely enough, caused a change in my attitude toward the Lost Dutchman Mine. Prior to this time, I had always felt there were far too many solid treasure leads right in my own back yard, so to speak, for me to chase elusive rainbows in other states; particularly the Lost Dutchman Mine. After all, everyone *knew* it was nothing more than an elaborate myth and I was in total accord with them. Nevertheless, I became fascinated with the area and knew I wanted to spend some time there but felt I must have a legitimate excuse. So it was then I began research on the famed lost mine, – not because I had even the slightest hope of it ever paying off monetarily, or even with the idea of trying to prove or disprove the legend, but merely as an excuse that would allow me to return, time and time again, to those intriguing mountains.

To my amazement, shortly after my study began I discovered there was far more involved than Jacob Walzer and his lost mine. One thing led to another and for the following three years I found myself avidly pouring over books and reports covering subjects that I never dreamed would be involved. At one point, all the information seemed to be nothing more than a monstrous compilation of bits and pieces of data that fit no place, but one thing was obvious – there was too much smoke for there to be no fire.

Eventually, and very slowly, order began to take form in the midst of chaos and, one by one, the pieces of the puzzle began to fall into place. Finally, I had an answer that, right or wrong, satisfied me, and when it comes to the Lost Dutchman Mine, that is about all for which one can even hope. Perhaps someday, information that will actually prove or disprove the stories of the mountain's wealth will come to light, but, to date, if any such information exists it is unknown to me.

When the research was completed, my field trips into the mountains began. While they have thus far failed to actually prove my theories correct, they have added substance to them, and all were very worthwhile. Several interesting discoveries have been made, including Spanish markings that, as far as I know, have never been reported or recorded. But, by far the most exciting of all the discoveries made, happened quite by accident; we found a mine! A very old mine.

On this particular trip we were camped on Tortilla Creek just east of Tortilla Mountain. We had completed the explorations planned for the trip and found ourselves with an extra day before we had to head for home. After discussing the possibilities and the best way to put the time to good use, we decided to explore the region in the immediate area of our camp. A few days before, we had noticed a cave high on the side of a mountain just east of our camp and wondered what an investigation of it would produce. We made that our goal.

The mountain appeared to be an easy climb. It sloped gently upward for about two-thirds of the way and supported much vegetation. The top one-third of the mountain where the cave was located was comprised of a massive rock formation that seemed to have forced its rugged head up through the otherwise gently sloping mountain. Nevertheless, we expected no problems in reaching our cave. This proved to be an erroneous assumption. Once we reached the base of the rock formation that formed the top one-third of the mountain, we realized that in order to reach the cave, we would have to go all the way to the top and work our way down to it. Having spent close to an hour getting that far, we felt there had been too much energy spent to turn back. We carefully began to work our way up.

As we were climbing to the top, we noticed the rock was interlaced with thin seams of white quartz; the first mineralization of that type we had noticed in that region of the Superstition area. Needless to say, this triggered considerable discussion.

When we finally reached the top of the mountain the view was breathtaking! To the north there was the famed Four Peaks boldly outlined against the sky. To the east was Tortilla Mountain with the Old Spanish Trail plainly visible running along its base. To the south, we could see the tops of several peaks but were unable to ascertain whether or not one of them was Weavers Needle. And, strangely, to the east, instead of the mountain being steep and rocky as was the western face that we had climbed, it slopped downward into gently rolling hills upon which tall green grass frew in profusion. It was a very surprising sight.

After a few minutes rest, we began to look for a way to get down to the cave and finally selected a water crevice as the safest and easiest way. But even this proved to be tricky. We had descended not more than 25 or 30 feet, before we had to leave the crevice and begin to work our way around toward the western face of the mountain in the direction of the cave. We had just worked our way around a large bounder when we ran smack into the entrance of a tunnel.

The first thought was that it was our cave, but we realized it was much too close to the top of the mountain, and faced the wrong direction. Instead of facing west as the cave did, this opening faced northwest and overlooked a small ravine. The same thought occurred to all of us simultaneously and we wasted no time getting into the tunnel to look it over.

The tunnel was about eight feet in diameter and extended back into the mountain approximately 40 to 50 feet. One of the most interesting things that we noticed first was a hole in the top of the tunnel that penetrated all the way through to the top of the mountain. This hole was about three to four feet in diameter and was located about eight or ten feet from the entrance to the tunnel. It admitted enough light to illuminate the interior of the tunnel making investigation easy and pleasant. We were unable to definitely establish whether the hole had somehow been formed by nature, or if it was man-made.

Careful examination of the walls of the tunnel revealed tell-tale signs of having been worked with a pick. There was one shaft that penetrated the right side of the tunnel and ran back into the tunnel near its end. Try as we might, we could not determine what type of ore had been taken from the mine. Nor did careful search with metal detectors produce anything.

Back on the outside, we could now see what was left of the dump. In fact, we were standing on it, but it was all but indistinguishable due to erosion and the ample amount of brush that now grew there. Had we not known a mine to be there, we would have never realized we were standing on an old dump. It was then that we realized the tunnel was naturally hidden by the contours of the mountain and that you had to be right on top of it to know it was there.

The next hour or so was spent sitting in the entrance of the tunnel discussing the pros and cons of whether or not this could possibly be the famed, long-sought lost mine.

It was located high on the side of a mountain and was naturally hidden. You could see the canyon below from the mine, but you could not see the mine from the canyon below. While it was not the old Military Trail in the canyon below, there was the Old Spanish Trail still plainly visible. It was but a short climb to the top of the mountain from which peaks (perhaps one of them Weavers Needle) could be seen to the south. The grassy pasture-like area on the eastern side of the mountain fit the description of an area near the mine where Walzer and his partner would hobble their horses while they worked the mine. We knew of no cave in the mountain across the ravine from the mine, but there was one below the mine. And, there was a shaft, or hole, running from the top of the tunnel all the way to the top of the mountain (could it at one time have been a cone-shaped pit?). It wasn't long before we had built ourselves quite a case!

It suddenly occurred to us that the day was getting away, and that we still had not reached our original goal; the cave. It took but a few minutes to get the rest of the way down to it. In exploring it we found it to be shallow and extending back into the mountain only about eight feet. The only thing interesting about it was evidence of fires indicating that it had been used by man sometime in the past.

After a few minutes we began our climb back to the top of the mountain, pausing briefly to have one last look at "our" mine.

Back at camp and away from the influence of our exciting discovery we began to think more clearly. As difficult as it was for us to admit, and in spite of the fact that the mine was located within the specified radius we had established, we faced the fact that while "our" mine did meet many of the requirements, it did not meet them all. We concluded that it was probably nothing more than a prospect that someone, perhaps the Spaniards, had dug. Probably following some of the thin seams of quartz hoping they might run into something. Regardless, we could not find even the slightest trace of gold. And, if there was ever any there, it had been completely worked out. Nevertheless, it was a richly rewarding experience and one that I will never forget.

Since then, I have often chuckled when reading some reports of various individuals who say they have found the Lost Dutchman Mine and explain the lack of gold by stating that it has been worked out. They "know" beyond a doubt that the mine they found is "it" because the locale, etc., fits some of the Dutchman's clues. Evidently, they were overcome with the similarities and failed to consider the aspects that were not favorable. It was with these reports in mind that I dubbed the mine we found as the LDM, Jr.

For anyone who might be interested in visiting the mine, it is located, as previously described, high on the side of a mountain which is located east of Tortilla Mountain on the east side of Tortilla Creek, and about one and one-half mile south of Tortilla Ranch. Trying to explain how to find the mine itself is somewhat difficult because, as previously stated, you cannot see it until you are upon it. Simply climb to the top of the mountain by whatever route seems to be easiest for you. Once on top, search around the northwestern edge for a water crevice that affords a fairly safe way down. Follow this for about 25 to 30 feet and then begin to work your way around toward the western face of the mountain. If you are on the right track, you will have to drop down about four feet to the base of a large boulder. Just on the other side of this boulder, you will find the entrance to the mine.

I must caution you, however, not to attempt to go there alone. There are places where a slip of the foot could be disastrous. There are also numerous rattlesnakes in this particular area and one should be on a constant lookout for them.

Having brushed on the subject of some of the dangers involved in making a trip into the Superstition area it might be well to deal with this facet of the picture a little more thoroughly. Almost everything that has ever been written regarding the Superstition Mountains invariably includes formidable and, sometimes, ominous warnings. While there is a need for admonitions, the area is not actually so different from any other rugged desert area.

The beauty of the remote regions is without equal. Instead of an unfriendly and hostile atmosphere, I have found the mountains to be peaceful and a delightful retreat, and have thoroughly enjoyed every trip. This is not to say that one can safely journey into the Superstitions with no more thought or preparations than that necessary for a stroll through a park, for nothing could be further from the truth. There are dangers that most assuredly do exist, and one should be aware of them and prepare himself accordingly. Otherwise, his trip into the Superstitions might well be one from which he never returns alive.

First, if you are planning a trip into the Superstitions make sure of your water supply. The mountains are not normally as dry as many would lead you to believe. There are several permanent water sources, but you have to know where they are and how to get to them. Regardless of how long you plan to be in the mountains, figure out how much water you will need, and take twice that amount along. And, it should be remembered that the lack of humidity in this section of Arizona is such that you will consume at least twice as much water as you would in many other desert areas and many times the amount you would at home.

Another prerequisite for anyone who plans on straying from the well-marked trails is to obtain a topographic map of the area, learn to read it correctly, and take it with you. It is not at all difficult for the most seasoned desert rat to become confused and lost in the innermost regions of the area.

The entire region teams with wildlife, but, with a few exceptions, there is little to be feared from it. But, the animal life which is dangerous, is very dangerous, making it essential to be prepared and constantly on your toes. Make double sure that you have a snake-bite kit on your person at all times, as there is no shortage of rattlesnakes in the Superstitions. I have yet to make a trip there without encountering at least one. Be especially careful when you are near creeks or springs and in the waning hours of the afternoon. To wander about at night is sheer folly!

Tarantulas, centipedes, and scorpions are also abundant, but while their bites are painful, they are not deadly. That is, with one exception; the bite of the small yellow scorpion can be fatal. This scorpion differs from his brothers, and can be identified from them by the fact that the segments of his tail are long and slender like a grain of rice, instead of being more round as with other species of scorpion. Fortunately, the deadly species is rare, but the sting of this creature requires prompt medical attention and an antivenom. And, as in almost every other area of the United States, there are Black Widow spiders, the bite of which also requires prompt medical attention.

The species of large animals that inhabit the mountains include deer, bobcats, mountain lions, javalinas, coyotes, and, according to some, bear. Generally speaking, none of them are dangerous to man unless molested and all are protected by the United States Government and the State of Arizona. However, the javalina has been known to attack man without provocation and their actions cannot be depended on. If one, or a pack, is encountered, your best bet is to ignore it and hope that it, too, ignores you. But, be prepared in case it does not.

Probably the most dangerous of all the animals that may be encountered in the Superstition area is the same one that is the most dangerous regardless of where you are — — — man. But, this is especially true in these mountains, and particularly in and around the Weavers Needle area. Here, there are recluses and other individuals who have claims, with each one of them feeling sure they are on the verge of finding the Lost Dutchman Mine. To some of these characters anyone trespassing in their domain is a threat, and the fact that their claims are not always posted, will not stop them from taking pot shots at you. It is true that most of this shooting is intended to go over your head, and merely frighten you away, but this writer, for one, does not have that much confidence in their marksmanship. Should you encounter such a situation, or if someone approaches you and tells you to leave, don't argue with them! Leave the area immediately, and if you have been shot at or threatened with a gun, report it to the local authorities.

The Superstitions are also used as a disappearing place for many, who, for one reason or another, are running away from trouble or the police. A good rule to follow, is to be friendly, offer help when needed, but be forever on your guard.

As when going into any remote area, it is well to be armed when making a trip into the Superstitions, but keep your gun holstered unless it is an actual matter of self-defense, be it a threat from snakes, animals, or otherwise.

Above all, before you go into the mountains, check in with the local sheriff. Tell him where you are going to be camped and the areas you intend to explore. Give him a definite time and date you plan to return. Then, upon your return, check in again and let him know you made it out safely. If this is done, and you should run into trouble, you can rest assured that when you do not appear on schedule, a search party will be out looking for you. And, if you get lost, stay put!

As a final word here, it should be pointed out that trips simply should not be made during the summer months. October, November, March, and April have proven to be excellent months to go. And, make sure you stay out of the mountains during hunting season. It is usually of no more than ten days duration, and it would be far better to postpone your trip for a few days, than risk going into the mountains when the hunters are 'out'. Anyone who is not experienced with desert and mountain conditions, is incapable of handling emergencies, or is not in good physical condition should stay out of the Superstitions all together. And, *NEVER* go into the mountains alone!

Chapter Fifteen

GOLD

The Lost Dutchman Mine has been the target for hundreds of adventurous men and women for almost a century, and while none of them have yet found Jacob Walzer's fabulous and elusive mine, there have been a few who did find gold in the Superstition Mountains. There were the two old men, Goldlock and Silverlock, who recovered over $15,000 in gold from the massacre site. Then, in the mid-1940's, there was the group of men who discovered a fantastic amount of gold stashed in a cave near the northern perimeter of the Superstition area. To my knowledge, these are the only two finds involving an appreciable amount of gold that are definitely authentic. But there have been reports of others, some bearing a certain amount of credibility.

In 1894, a man named Waggoner allegedly discovered and worked a rich gold-bearing deposit of rose quartz that was believed to be located in the area just west of Picacho Butte. There is supposed to be a circle of trees planted by Waggoner marking the site of the rich outcropping which he kept carefully concealed with rocks and brush.

A rose quartz float, rich in gold, was found in 1952 near the west side of Picacho Butte. This float assayed out at $20,000 per ton. The report of this find comes from a very reliable source and certainly adds considerable credence to the Waggoner story in spite of the fact that many have prospected and searched the area without success.

It has also been reported that several individuals have found gold-bearing float in the Boulder Canyon area. But, try as they might, they were unable to locate an outcropping from which they could have come. It might be well to mention at this point, that there are rumors to the effect that the popular Weavers Needle area and nearby canyons were once 'salted' with gold ore. The object of this deception was supposedly to help facilitate the sale of worthless claims to unwary victims. If this is true, no doubt this attempted swindle operation accounts for some, if not all, of the rich floats found in these areas.

There have been a few reports of individuals locating placer deposits in the Superstitions. In 1879 two Mexicans were climbing up the side of the mountain when they reportedly found a large deposit of black sand and gold in a gulch. Some particles of the gold were said to be the size of a pea. While recovering a portion of the gold, they were attacked by Indians. Only one of the men managed to escape and return to civilization. He was never able to find the location again.

Along with this, there are several reports stating that there are certain portions of Tortilla Creek that have produced placer gold; as recently as the mid-1960's, in fact.

While the Lost Dutchman is by far the most famous, there is another lost mine that is said to be located in the Superstitions. Like most lost mines, the possibility of the actual existence of this one is very slim. Nevertheless, it is an interesting possibility and like so many other tales of gold in the Superstitions, this one comes from the Indians.

According to the legend, many years ago a group of armor-clad Spaniards journeyed into the Superstition Mountains and located a fabulous deposit of gold in a small sunken valley located on the top of a mountain. The only way to get in and out of this valley was to use ropes to scale the steep walls that completely enclosed it.

They worked the deposit and made friends with the Indians by giving them trinkets. In return, the Indians would sometimes bring them freshly-killed game. They labored for many months, taking the gold from the mountain. After smelting it into bars, they would store them in a near-by cave. All went well until the day when one of the Spaniards raped an Indian girl. This was unforgivable, and, to the Indians way of thinking, if it happened once, it could happen again. So, they decided to destroy the entire group of Spaniards.

To accomplish this, they chose a uniquely morbid method. The braves surrounded the rim of the little valley and shot arrows at the Spaniards until they had them cornered in a small area. Then, they proceeded to crush them to death by pushing boulders down on top of them.

With the job completed, they left the bodies lying where they fell and gave no thought to the bars of gold stacked in the cave. The Indians say that everything there, is still as it was the day the Spanish miners were wiped out. They maintain there is very little chance the little valley will ever be found by white men because it is naturally hidden and located in an out-of-the-way place. To the Indians, the area is taboo.

If, by chance, there is any truth to this legend, there is quite a discovery awaiting someone. In fact, according to one report, a valley fitting the description of the one in the legend was accidentally found by a man on a hiking trip in the 1920's. He said he used a rope to get down to the valley floor and while exploring it found ruins of an old Spanish encampment along with several objects that date back several centuries. But he had never heard the tale of the Spaniard's sunken valley and their gold operations there, so he failed to give the matter much thought at the time.

The man also said that he found a cave and followed it through the mountain to an opening on the other side. If he saw any stacks of gold bars in the cave, the report does not mention it.

Another source gives a little different version of the story of the Spanish miners and states that the old Apache warlord, Geronimo, was aware of this valley and knew the location of the gold that was stored there. Geronimo reportedly said that the valley is located on the mountain between Peters Canyon and La Barge Canyon near Tortilla Flat. This mountain is today known as Geronimo Head.

Along with the tales of lost mines, there are several stories of vast treasures that are supposed to be secreted in the Superstitions. There is one canyon that has, through the years, been known by several names. Even today there is considerable disagreement as to its location. It was once known as the Spanish Aversion Canal Canyon. Another name that some reports use is Peralta Canyon (not the same one that is located on the southern side of the mountains and is so well-known today), and still others refer to it Skeleton Canyon. Some say it is located near the Mormon Flat Dam, and that a portion of it is now under the waters of Canyon Lake. Others maintain it is situated just east of Fish Creek near Castle Dome Mountain. Wherever it is and regardless of its name, it is said to be the depository of a fortune in gold.

The value of this treasure, which allegedly is in the form of gold bars weighing 100 pounds each, is said to be over $5,000,000. It is supposed to be a portion of a treasure that was brought from Mexico in the early years of the 19th century.

There are a surprising number of no-nonsense people who believe in this particular treasure. Some who believe the canyon in question is partly underwater at Canyon Lake, have spent considerable time and money engaging in skin diving operations attempting to locate a cave at the base of what once was a waterfall where the treasure is supposed to be hidden. If they are correct as to the canyon's location, and if the story is true, there is very little chance the gold will ever be recovered. The waters of Canyon Lake are very muddy in places, making underwater exploration very difficult. Even if anyone should locate what was once a waterfall, it is doubtful they would ever be able to get into the cave if one does exist there. Considering the length of time Canyon Lake has been in existence, chances are that the entrance to the cave is now covered by many feet of mud and sediment.

So far as it is known, search of the area east of Fish Creek near Castle Dome Mountain where some people believe the canyon is located has failed to produce anything. It seems that there should be some way to at least establish the location of the canyon in question, but the available information is contradictory in this respect.

While there are very few details known, the Apaches are said to have a vast treasure hidden in the Superstition area. This cache is reportedly worth millions and is supposed to be hidden in the Black Cross Butte area. According to some sources, it is this hoard of gold that the mysterious band of Apaches known as the Black Legion is guarding. The gold is said to be hidden in a cave near the old Indian burial grounds. Unfortunately, or perhaps fortunately, depending on the validity of the reports concerning the Black Legion, no one seems to know the exact location of these sacred burial grounds. Even the old-timers have different opinions as to its location. One report places both the burial grounds and Skeleton Canyon in the same area;

approximately two miles south of the Salt River and north of Black Cross Butte.

Another story involving still other treasures comes from the Indians, too, but is of more recent vintage. Instead of one large cache, numerous small ones are said to be buried in the region south of the old Tortilla Ranch. They were hidden around the turn of this century by small renegade bands of Apaches who had hideouts in this area. The members of these bands were eventually tracked down and either killed or captured without ever being able to return and recover the riches they had so carefully concealed.

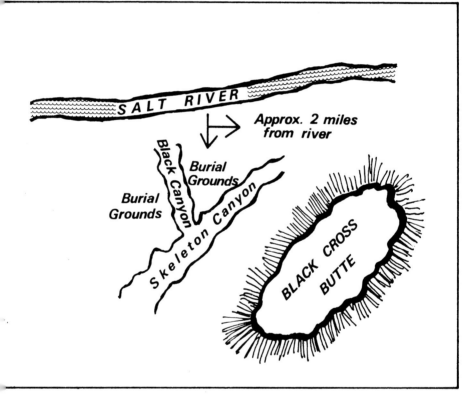

ILLUSTRATION G: Sketch of one reported location of the Apache burial grounds and Skeleton Canyon. Each is supposedly the site where a vast treasure is hidden.

In the early years of the 1950's, two men did, in fact, locate a sizable cache of gold in this area and returned two weeks later in the dead of night and recovered it. But this involved only one cache. There should be others.

Then, of course, there is the treasure known in some circles as the Hidalgo treasure, that many believe was brought into the mountains by the Peraltas. This treasure is supposed to be in the form of ingots and native gold, and is said to be worth millions. It is from this treasure that many believe Jacob Walzer obtained his gold. And, there are some who believe that the famed Maximillian treasure is hidden in the Superstitions.

Actually, there is almost no end to the rumors, stories, and legends of gold that is said to be secreted in the Superstition Mountains. Even if one-half of them are true, no doubt the Superstitions would contain more gold than Ft. Knox, back in the good old days when the depository actually held the gold we would all like to think it still does. Of course, it is foolish to entertain the thought of all these stories being true. Or, even a good part of them, for that matter. There simply is not enough available information at this time to stamp any of them 100% authentic and true. On the other hand, though it may have nothing to do with any of these stories, a fortune in gold has, indeed, been found and recovered in the Superstition area. This proves that at least one group of individuals selected the region as a safe hiding place for their gold. If one did, why not another?

Chapter Sixteen

...The Omega

It has been over 80 years since the death of Jacob Walzer, but, without a doubt, there are as many people searching for his mine now, as there were shortly after his death. From time to time, shreds, bits, and pieces of information, come to light, some of which would seem to be helpful. But, after studying and delving into it, it is almost invariably laid aside with the hope that someday it will be possible to put it to use. The enigma of the Lost Dutchman Mine is indeed a puzzle with many missing pieces, and for all practical purposes, is no closer to being solved now, than it was 80 years ago.

There are many theories as to why this is the case. One, which is widely believed by those who have never bothered to study the matter or were unable to accept defeat when they could not find it, is that the Dutchman's gold never existed at all, except in the imagination of storytellers. Another belief is that Walzer worked it out himself, and that there is nothing remaining to be found. Then, there are those who believe that Walzer did have a gold source in the mountains, but disagree vehemently as to what it was — cache or mine. Some of them believe that it is still there, waiting for anyone who has enough ingenuity to find it.

The controversy rages on and on, and seemingly cannot be resolved. At least not completely. Perhaps the Lost Dutchman Mine *is* non-existent. But, if so, it is only because it is non-existent as many people who believe in the legend think of it as being.

If the enigma of the Lost Dutchman Mine had to be described in a single word, 'frustrating' would be the most fitting. It is doubtful that there is any lost mine or tale of buried treasure that is more well-known or has had more written about it. Thousands upon thousands of words have been set down by dozens of authors on the subject, and thousands of people have searched for it.

While much of the information does not coincide, and in some instances, seems contradictory, enough of it is well-founded, to make it most difficult for one not to give the subject serious consideration. It would be a simple matter if the stories and legends were so full of holes that one could research them and label them "fictitious" and forget them. But this is not the case. There is one fact that cannot be disputed. Over one-quarter of a million dollars in gold passed through Jacob Walzer's hands. Where did he get it?

Did he find it in the cave where the group of men in the 1940's discovered a king's ransom in gold? Or, was it another cache that he stumbled upon. Perhaps he had a map he used that enabled him to find it. Could it be that his gold came from the western slope of the mountain where the two strange old men, Silverlock and Goldlock, found their gold in the early part of this century? Maybe it came from one of the old Spanish mines that are known to exist near Goldfield. There are several possible solutions including the most enticing of all: perhaps, somewhere in the rugged Superstitions, possibly covered by nothing more than a few inches of overburden or merely concealed by undergrowth, there is one of the richest gold mines in the world.

After careful consideration, it becomes apparent that those who believe the Dutchman's gold came from a cache, and those who maintain it came from an actual mine, have good and sound reasons for their beliefs. Regardless of the way the evidence may stack up indicating it was a cache, there is nothing to actually prove this to be the case. Nor is there any evidence proving it was a mine. But, there is ample evidence indicating that both rich mines and caches have existed in the Superstition area, and perhaps, still do.

In the final analysis, the only individuals who are totally in error regarding the Lost Dutchman Mine are those who maintain that the Dutchman and his gold are nothing more than legend. Jacob Walzer was very real, and so was his gold . . . *all $250,000 worth!*

EPILOGUE

Is the gold-magnet strong enough? Does it threaten to shred your mind into a thousand minute sections, or do you believe the Lost Dutchman Mine and its petrifying legends of death to be mere folly?

If the latter be true, there's a place — 35 miles east of Phoenix — which might go a long way to converting you into a supporter, if not a lender, to the LDM legend. It's called Apache Junction, Arizona. But eight miles (yes, and eight minutes) away lie the Superstitions . . .

The author and I trudged up Peralta Canyon trail one weekend to shoot most of the photographs contained in this work. And, if any fool thinks he is smart enough to buy a map, hike right in and then find Walzer's bonanza, either he had better be old Jacob's grandson, or have very tough feet.

The Superstitions are as incredibly beautiful as they are difficult to hike. After a half-mile, you expect Geronimo himself to jump from behind a boulder, pull a knife, and stake you out. One look, and it must be in person, is enough to tell you why the mine has yet to be found. Then, I am sure, one look will turn into another, then another, until there is never "a last trip" into the Superstitions. The mountains literally (and sometimes audibly) challenge you to enter them and succeed where thousands have failed.

One thing is certain: these mountains are dangerous . . . and man makes them so. While we were shooting pictures, others were shooting rifles and pistols all around us. It wasn't exactly Viet Nam, but the camera was shaking enough, so much so, I once wondered if we could ever get back, much less get this book into print.

But enough of this editor's tom-foolery.

Estee has written a very, very good book. Editors do not like to say excellent, for then they have nothing with which to work . . . for then they are no longer required. But this is as close to "excellent" which will ever come out of the treasure hunting field, unless Mrs. Conatser decides to write about her own theories concerning the location of the famous mine.

And a theory she has, in a *THEORY* way. Estee merely did not wish to burden you, the reader, with another author's theory — — — she wants you to make that decision, your own theory. And why not? The facts, the map, they are all here. Two or three careful readings and you can come up with the most probable location of the LDM.

If there is one person who *might* know where Jacob's mine is, Estee Conatser is that person. Whether or not she finds it, remains lost into the future.

But perhaps, one day, I can tell my kids I once knew the person who wrote about and found the famous mine. And you can tell your kids you knew her too.

For Estee Conatser is this book. Please read it again, and get to know her better. It's as rewarding as your first view of Weaver's Needle.

Apache Junction, Arizona　　　　　　　　　　*Robert Morehead III*
September 3, 1972.　　　　　　　　　　　　　*Ram Publishing Co.*